THE GREAT GARDENS OF CHINA

HISTORY · CONCEPTS · TECHNIQUES

FANG XIAOFENG

THE MONACELLI PRESS

CONTENTS

FOREWORD

Chinese gardens are often considered intellectual abstractions, too rarefied to be understood by the ordinary gardener. For me, however, they are a set of brilliant solutions to almost every major garden problem. There are formal rules, but these can be broken; there are a variety of styles, but these can be adapted on a mix-and-match basis; and although most of the gardens seem impossibly old, they are constantly renewing themselves.

They have also deeply influenced the most avant garde of garden designers. Near my very traditional garden in southwest Scotland is The Garden of Cosmic Speculation. This extraordinary project has been created over the last twenty years by Charles Jencks and Maggie Keswick Jencks. Maggie knew China well, was entranced by Chinese gardens, and did a great deal to bring them and their inherent philosophy to the West. It was a great privilege to know her briefly before her untimely death.

Although the garden she and her husband made together is based on science and mathematics, it took its original inspiration from Chinese gardens, and their spirit runs through this wonderful work of art. Even the rather whimsical name fits the Chinese mold.

Take too, the incomparable Chinese-American architect, I. M. Pei. He spent his childhood in one of the most glorious of China's classical gardens, the Lion Grove in Suzhou: it was his family home until he left for Harvard University in 1935. Almost seventy years later he designed the deeply satisfying Suzhou Museum next door to the old family home. It is a building where there is no division between interior and exterior. There is no feeling of inside and outside; it is not a garden with a museum or a museum with a garden. As in the best Chinese gardens, buildings and garden meld into one.

I. M. Pei oversaw every step of the creation of the museum gardens, even choosing individual trees. Although the end result is entirely classical in concept, consisting of rock, water, trees, bamboo, and paving, it is at the same time utterly modern. Unlike some re-creations of Chinese gardens it never descends into pastiche. It is rather a classical Chinese garden for a new century.

I have written about these two new gardens at some length because to Western eyes, China almost seems to have an excess of history. And once things are consigned to history, they seem to lose any relevance for the here and now. I feel very strongly that despite their great age, these gardens should not be looked upon as museum pieces. In order to appreciate them, we may have to adjust our attitudes and lose a few of our preconceptions about what a garden should be, but surely new perspectives are always a good idea. We may not like or understand everything that we see, but that's fine too—I don't like or understand everything I see in Western gardens either.

I am writing this sitting in the Xiling Seal Engravers' Society by the West Lake in Hangzhou, China, having visited some of the gardens featured in this book. It was wonderful to experience the gardens I had always dreamed of seeing, but it was not without its frustrating side. I longed to sit alone in a waterside pavilion in the moonlight listening to the breeze in the bamboo and the splash of a rising fish. Or to watch the lotus flowers unfurl in the cool of early morning when everything is fresh with dew. Sadly, the modern visitor's experience does not allow for such indulgences.

But this book allows a less frustrating experience. It is a total immersion in the enticing art of Chinese classical gardens. The pictures capture the essence of each garden, and in writing the captions I have tried to include both what I could see, and also that extra element that the photographer has miraculously caught. The author of the text, Fang Xiaofeng, has helped me greatly to understand how Chinese gardens work and how to borrow from them for our own gardens in the West. In fact, you don't even need to have a garden at all. A pot of bamboo casting its shadow on a white wall can be as potent as a lakeside pavilion.

Janet Wheatcroft
Craigieburn Garden
Moffat
Scotland

ORIGIN AND EVOLUTION

Thus a garden was created as an art form whereby educated people could express their ideas and feelings. Over the centuries, the Chinese garden developed its own logic and its own language. Gardens, in Chinese culture, have always been more than simple combinations of flowers, trees, and miniature landscapes; they are places that can create poetic and painterly concepts.

The Chinese World View

Classical Chinese gardens have evolved and changed over the centuries, their cultural connotations growing deeper and richer over time. In fact, the traditional Chinese garden left a deep impression on China's neighboring countries, including Japan and South Korea. Equally, it thrilled visiting European traders and missionaries who, on returning home, enlightened their fellow Europeans about China and its gardens.

The Chinese garden is a complex and intriguing element of China's rich cultural heritage, and perhaps for these reasons, has roused the interest of garden-art lovers in both modern China and beyond. Gardens have had so significant an impact on the aesthetic ideals of the Chinese people that their pervasive influence is still strong today. The essence of the Chinese garden derives from a traditional philosophy, developed as a synthesis of the constant opposition in Taoist philosophy between Tao and qi, or the tension between the intangible (metaphysical) and the tangible (physical). In this fundamental pair of concepts, qi refers to all the things in nature that can be perceived by the senses, while Tao is the origin from which all things are generated.

Thus a garden was created as an art form whereby educated people could express their ideas and feelings. Over the centuries, the Chinese garden developed its own logic and its own language. Gardens, in Chinese culture, have always been more than simple combinations of flowers, trees, and miniature landscapes; they are places that can create poetic and painterly concepts (Fig. 1). For cultured people, gardens were distinctive markers of elite status. No man could be considered a true intellectual without a garden of his own, be it large or small. By the same token, no room would be perfect as a study unless its owner might look out of the window and see his own exquisite garden of strangely shaped rocks and fantastic looking plants (Fig. 2). Since classical Chinese gardens closely resemble the classical paintings produced by this educated elite, they are also regarded as a kind of three-dimensional landscape painting or "solid poetry."

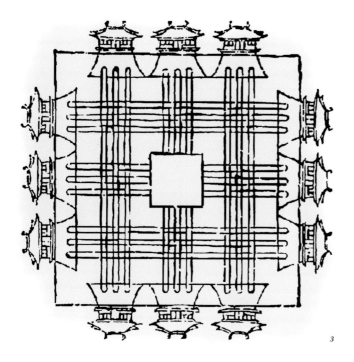

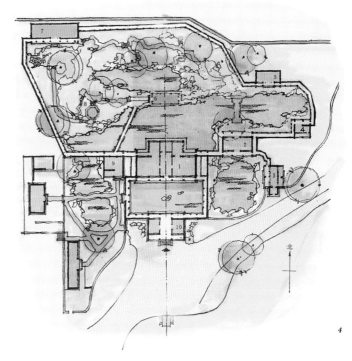

The Garden and the City

Fig. 3 A stylized drawing of the captial city explaining the strict architectural plan, recorded in Kaogongji (Records of Techniques) (Zhou Dynasty).

Fig. 4 The plan of the Heart-Ease Study, in Beijing, overlooking water: it shows the relative freedom inherent in Chinese garden design.

The early 17th- and 18th-century European missionaries in China contrasted European with Chinese cities. In the West, cities were built in many different styles, while Chinese cities tended to be built to a single dominant pattern. In the West, noble and royal gardens were often on a grand scale, dominated by formal parterres and a rigid geometry (Fig. 3). In China gardens were more private, peaceful and secluded, filled with winding paths, hidden away from the city and the public gaze. However, within the architectural uniformity of a Chinese city, the gardens were the places of retreat, where officials, intellectuals, or even emperors could retire from the pressures of everyday life. In the tranquility of the garden they could fulfill their yearning for freedom (Fig. 4).

In China as elsewhere, most gardens were designed to bridge the divide between architecture and the surrounding landscape. Gardens represented a bridge between man and nature, a concept which ultimately became a common feature in gardens around the world. Often within a garden, its structure and organization suggested an ideal, inflected by an individual's perception of the world and subtly exemplifying the relationship between man and nature. Classical Chinese gardens strongly reflected these dualities. They were suffused with the worship of nature implicit in traditional Chinese culture. Rocks, lakes, flowers, and trees were all personified or endowed with spiritual meanings. Yet, over the years, landscape design and plant selection began to suggest less these traditional symbols and more the character and taste of garden owners.

Early Chinese scholars had likened making a garden to writing an essay—to making a concrete intellectual statement. So the Yonghe Lamasery, the residence of Emperor Yongzheng (1722–1735) of the Qing Dynasty (1616–1911), was dominated by a tall stone slab (stele) inscribed in Han Chinese, Manchu, Mongolian, and Tibetan languages on the divine nature of the empire, designed to highlight imperial power and majesty.

Over time, garden styles changed, both in China and in the West. The profusion of buildings that had marked early Chinese gardens was by the Qing Dynasty in the 17th century becoming less popular. Western gardens, too, were altering, using garden buildings in a new way, as isolated focal points, and sometimes these buildings—pagodas, temples, and other traditional buildings—were Chinese in origin. Fine examples in England were the Chinese Pagoda (1762) in the Royal Palace of Kew and the Chinese Dairy (1780) at the great ducal house of Woburn. The European style known as Chinoiserie was clear evidence of an intense Western curiosity about China's culture and artifacts. Sir William Chambers, who designed the great Pagoda, visited China to see its architecture for himself. How much he understood the philosophical roots of Chinese design is open to discussion, but the admiration for Chinese style cannot be questioned.

The traditional design of gardens in China had always emphasized an essential harmony between architecture and the environment; but during the Qing period gardens focused increasingly on the integration of natural beauty and craftsmanship rather than on individual elements. Tang Dynasty poet Bai Juyi (772–846) had probably been the first to define the composition of the various elements within a garden. Although not exactly a golden rule, generations of garden designers established the underlying principles of coordination within a garden: while individual cases might differ, the underlying patterns remained roughly the same.

Creating the Big Picture from the Small Detail

Within a sense of basic order, Chinese gardens display highly diversified forms. To enhance garden views, architectural elements and nature were blended in such a way as to present unique visual effects. In both the imperial and private gardens, the buildings display a rich variety of appearance, style, and scale, both horizontally and vertically. Their mass compositions often seem to anticipate the principles of European modernism. In effect, they "play the same tune but on different musical instruments." The spirit of freedom inherent in traditional Chinese gardens echoes the drive of Western modernism to break free from the constraints of early-20th-century architectural design.

In recent times, these garden styles, surprisingly, have found their way into public architecture. The Fragrant Hill Hotel in Beijing and the Suzhou Museum (Figs. 5–6) are two major projects in China by the Chinese-born and American-educated master architect I. M. Pei (b. 1917). Both were modeled after the principles of classical Chinese gardens; the garden

as a source of inspiration perhaps came naturally to Pei, for his family had once owned the famous Shizi-Lin (Lion Grove), one of the finest classical gardens in Suzhou of Eastern China's Jiangsu province. While still a student at Harvard, I. M. Pei had submitted an unsuccessful proposal to construct the China Art Museum in Shanghai. This design was again a garden-style plan, since he argued that this was the only way to guarantee a perfect atmosphere in which to view ancient Chinese artifacts.

Chinese painting and calligraphy do not usually require an exceptionally large space for collection and display, but they do demand a comfortably elegant setting to create the right mood (Fig. 7). After all, garden buildings were intended to heighten the perception of exquisite objects, to maximize their artistic

Fig. 5 The arrangement and layout of stones, designed by I. M. Pei in the Suzhou Museum, is inspired by Mi Fu's landscape painting (Song Dynasty).

Fig. 6 The view of the main exhibition hall from the courtyard in the Suzhou Museum, where bamboo plays an important role in terms of site and space. Pei's garden is a modern masterpiece, a brilliant reuse of the age-old classic principles in the modern era.

Fig. 7 Colorful carp in the lake in front of the Mingse Building of the Lingering Garden in Suzhou bring life and movement to a tranquil garden.

Fig. 8 In the Garden of Cultivation, Suzhou, looking south across the pool; the water places a necessary distance between the observer and the landscape.

expressiveness, and in some cases make these objects vie with each other for attention. So I. M. Pei's museum in the garden city of Suzhou uses garden motifs explicitly, with a garden and water within the white walls of the museum, and a wall of "thinly sliced rocks that echo a range of mountain peaks. The I. M. Pei project perfectly illustrates how the ancient traditions of Chinese garden design have a vital contemporary resonance. As he put it: "In China, architecture and the garden are one. A Western building is a building, and a garden is a garden: they are related in spirit. But in China they are one."

For the intellectuals of ancient China, forested hills were the best places to build gardens. Unfortunately real mountains and rivers were enormously costly and impractical to reconstruct in an urban environment. So the creators of ancient gardens used rocks and pools to express these elements symbolically. As an old Chinese saying goes, "Lower-class hermits live in

mountains; middle-class hermits in towns; upper-class hermits in the highest parts of the government." In his poem "Middle-Class Hermit," the Tang Dynasty poet Bai Juyi preaches the doctrine of Middle Way, a prime example closely followed by the literati in later centuries. Chinese gardens placed special emphasis on "creating the big picture from the small detail." The skill required of a garden designer was to create the effect of greater space and a broader view. In other words, the scene changes with each step you take, as the spectator becomes the observed: you are looking at the garden and at the same time you become part of the garden as others see you within it. Perhaps this is nowhere more dramatically presented than on the Broken Bridge that crosses the famous West Lake of Hangzhou in Zhejiang Province. Here the pedestrians using the bridge to cross the lake become part of the artistic spectacle for those viewing the bridge from the banks of the lake.

To stimulate the imagination, garden architects pay close attention to spatial effects and "borrowed landscapes," knowing that rigid boundaries would limit the sense of space and would stunt the imagination. This explains why most Chinese gardens straddle a hazy line between interior, domestic spaces, the "borrowed external landscape," and the "perfect object" for inspection and attention, like the exquisite rocks and stones in the finest traditional gardens. Indeed, a delicate balance between larger prospects and smaller detailed points of attention, can give the visitor the illusion of strolling through a natural forest.

Chinese gardens are "literary" in that they serve as expressions of an intellectual's feelings and ideas. To enjoy a Chinese garden and to understand the deeper meanings of rocks and pools (Fig. 8), visitors must let their minds and imaginations run free. The very word for landscape in Chinese means "mountains and water." Rocks, the quintessence of the mountain, for example, elicit a huge range of responses. They are symbolic both of mountains and of the most sublime human feelings. A fine rock must be slender and elegant, and open to rain and water cascading over its surface. It is not solid but pierced with apertures, cervices, and cavities, its surface creased and wrinkled by its long history. Sometimes it is almost possible to imagine it as a living object and not a geological specimen. Rocks were objects of love, especially the exquisite Taihu stones found only in the Lake Tai, west of Suzhou.

The Historical Development of Garden Design

Origins

Chinese gardens may be traced back to two origins: *yuanyou* and *lingtai*. In ancient China, the *yuanyou* was a sort of hunting ground, part wild and part cultivated. Within these spaces, Chinese emperors often built *lingtai*, massive towering platforms, like the European Tower of Babel, as a means to get closer to heaven and to communicate with deities (Fig. 9). There they made ritual offerings to the gods. *Lingtai* located within a *yuanyou* provided a fine example of how man-made architecture could be integrated into the natural environment, which would become the defining element of the Chinese garden. However, these proto-gardens were not intended for pleasure or entertainment, but served a strictly practical purpose.

Most people identify the emperor with a constant indulgence in pleasure, and so, in the Chinese view, imperial entertainments should be the most sublime in the world; many Chinese emperors were indeed highly inventive in creating new forms of delight. The development of classical Chinese gardens had much to do with those early emperors who, overjoyed at their escape from the confinement of palace walls, were entranced by the sights and sounds of the world beyond the palace. Properly constructed "natural" environments heightened the pleasure of walking in the garden. The panoramic view from a towering *lingtai* allowed people not only to communicate with heaven, but also to gaze down far into the distance—a delightful experience indeed. The *lingtai*, according to historians, looked massive and imposing, particularly those built in the Spring and Autumn Period (770–476 B.C.) and Warring States Period (476–221 B.C.), when it was extremely fashionable to build towering terraces and platforms, and splendid palaces and chambers. (A similar idea in Western gardens was the "mound," a ubiquitous feature of Elizabethan gardens in England. A winding path spiraled up around a man-made hill, allowing a panoramic view of the garden below.)

At that time, most palaces and gardens of the feudal princes were named after, and centered around, the high platforms, the landmarks that rose above the surrounding buildings. Among those platforms, Zhanghua, in today's Hubei province, was the grandest of these constructions. The palace of King Ling of Chu (540–529 B.C.), built in 535 B.C., Zhanghua was the first large-scale complex of terraced pavilions in ancient China. The tallest platforms (four different levels) once rose three stories to a height of 30 meters (98 feet). All visitors, it is said, would have to stop and rest three times before getting to the top, hence the name the Three-Rests Platform. Today, only the earth terraces remain.

Obviously, the earliest gardens were luxuries that few people could afford (Fig. 10). Most *yuanyou* were extremely large, usually stretching for miles. *Lingtai*, the means by which emperors and princes could make contact with heaven, were limited to them alone. Inside the *yuanyou*, the earliest gardens began to take shape; as time went on pleasure and entertainment displaced the religious elements, as the forms and functions of architecture within the garden became more and more varied. Over time the increasing number and variety of buildings and other structures provided new levels of comfort and stimulation to the imperial aesthetes. Perhaps the easiest way to understand these developments is chronologically.

Fig. 9 The Green Mountains by Anonymous (Yuan Dynasty).

Fig. 10 Carved stones showing a hunting scene or possibly a visit to a garden by a king (Eastern Han Dynasty).

019

Origin and Evolution

The Qin and Han Dynasties

Fig. 11 The Jianzhang Palace of the Han Dynasty is an important imperial garden, a place the emperor communicated with the deities.

Fig. 12 A fabled "abode of the immortals," one of the Forty Sights of Yuanmingyuan (Garden of Perfect Brightness), on the outskirts of Beijing. It was destroyed by the British and the French in 1860.

Fig. 13 The Thatched Cottage of Zhexi by Wu Hong (Qing Dynasty).

As soon as Shi Huangdi (221–210 B.C.), king of Qin, had defeated the other six warring states and unified China for the first time in its history, he began a vast building program of imperial palaces, often with gardens. Those listed in official records alone total as many as several hundred. But the Qin Dynasty (221–206 B.C.) lasted for no more than fifteen years before it was replaced by the long Han Dynasty (206 B.C.–210 A.D.). The earliest Han rulers inherited what remained of the Qin empire, and returned many of the more extensive gardens to farmland, or military training grounds. Since the water systems in these gardens were usually connected to water supply networks within the city walls, they were sometimes used by the emperors as an excuse to build imperial gardens (Fig. 11) with the explanation that they were "enhancing" the urban water supply facilities.

Since both Shi Huangdi and the Han Emperor Wudi (180–157 B.C.) intended to live forever, many structures and sites in their imperial gardens were constructed to represent the realm of the immortals. This practice exerted a profound impact on the garden makers of later dynasties, for legend has it that the immortals lived on a divine mountain in the middle of the sea. To re-create such an atmosphere, ancient architects would build three hills, or artificial islets, that faced each other within a lake or pool (Fig. 12). Similarly, high towers and grand pavilions were erected when the emperors learned that all the immortals lived in buildings of this type. As a result, most imperial gardens during this period were massive, splendid, and architecturally imposing.

The pursuit of immortality dominated every aspect of imperial life. Court alchemists elaborated complex

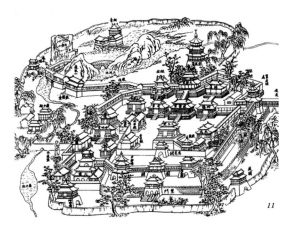

11

elixirs to prolong the emperor's existence. Huge bronze basins were placed on high pillars to gather dew, for the emperors were led to believe that regular use of jade powder mixed with dew would give them eternal life. As they sought immortality, other imperial duties were increasingly neglected, and toward the end of the Han Dynasty, widespread social unrest led to the disintegration of the centralized political system. One result was that the vast imperial gardens fell into disrepair until they were eventually divided up into smaller, private gardens.

The growing social turmoil led intellectuals to turn away from worldly concerns and to retire into a secluded life. Standing aloof from factional politics and the ceaseless competition for official government posts, the scholars chose to retreat into nature (Fig. 13), knowing that relative poverty and a retreat from the struggle for power might eventually save their lives. Private gardens, accordingly, were born not only to enhance comfort and provide solace, but also

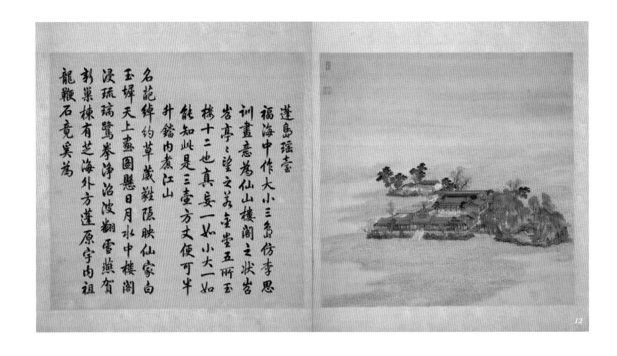

12

to enhance the deep-rooted traditions of seclusion. Escaping from the world, however, sometimes ran the risk of arousing suspicions among disbelieving government officials, often with fatal results. As a result, the intellectuals had to make it clear that they truly had no political ambitions, and that they genuinely preferred the lifestyle of complete tranquility, experiencing the solace of their gardens.

Wei, Jin, and Northern and Southern Dynasties

Fig. 14 A Leisurely and Carefree Mood *by Sun Wei (Tang Dynasty). The style of the Wei and Jin dynasties is evident as is the impact of the literati on gardens.*

Fig. 15 Preface of Lanting Pavilion Collection *by Wang Xizhi, a famous calligrapher of the Eastern Jin Dynasty.*

Following the Han came almost four hundred years of disunity with China split between local dynasties, ruling small kingdoms rather than a united imperial state. Not until the 5th century A.D. was a truly imperial power reborn. This historical context—constant insecurity, frequent shifts of power, and alien rule gave rise to two attitudes toward life: carpe diem and cynicism.

The former was manifest in an extremely extravagant lifestyle and a competitive display of wealth, while the latter produced a reclusive lifestyle of inwardness, metaphysical simplicity, narcissistic aloofness, and liberation of self. After the Jin Dynasty moved its capital to Southern China, the scholars came into a spectacular landscape, marking the birth of landscape art. The literati started viewing nature as something vital and dynamic, and hence a strong and equal relationship between man and nature was established. The Wei

(220–265) and Jin (265–420) intellectuals have always been regarded by later generations as the scholars, who loved dearly to surround themselves with nature. Carefree, easygoing, playful, and witty, they would gather in the great outdoors to debate freely on whatever issues interested them, or to compose and recite poems over wine (Fig. 14).

Buddhism, according to some historians, was first introduced into China during the Eastern Han period (25–220), but did not have much impact until the Northern and Southern Dynasties, when Buddhism began to flourish in China following the transfer of state power to local rulers. Meanwhile, enriched by the alien religion, the local Taoism was transformed, becoming more philosophically complex and sophisticated. The rapid spread of religions fueled the popularity of religious architecture. The new imposing temples and monasteries, in turn, added much appeal to Buddhism.

The growing popularity of temples and monasteries gave rise to temple gardens that closely resembled private gardens—where houses and gardens had become a united architectural form. Chinese temples and monasteries are, in essence, architecturally no different from ordinary buildings except for shape and size. The atmosphere created added a new dimension to the appeal of a religious life.

At the same time the imperial gardens had become smaller, but more elaborate and refined. Rocks and flowing water offered endless opportunities for artifice. The architects would stack rocks into artificial

永和九年歲在癸丑暮春之初
于會稽山陰之蘭亭脩禊事
也羣賢畢至少長咸集此地
有峻領（崇山）茂林脩竹又有清流激
湍暎帶左右引以為流觴曲水
列坐其次雖無絲竹管弦之
盛一觴一詠亦足以暢敘幽情
是日也天朗氣清惠風和暢仰
觀宇宙之大俯察品類之盛
所以遊目騁懷足以極視聽之
娛信可樂也夫人之相與俯仰
一世或取諸懷抱悟言一室之內
或曰寄所託放浪形骸之外雖

15

14

hills, striving for amazingly convoluted waterscapes. They devoted more and more attention to the mechanics of controlling water, developing remarkably innovative tools to create ever more elaborate water features. There had been a marked shift from creating an illusion of a divine presence to more worldly aspirations. The dynamic interaction between two cultures—that of the royal family and that of the educated commoners—gave a strong impetus to the development of garden art (Fig. 15). Historical records show that some intellectuals were employed by the royal household to maintain their gardens, evidence that the aesthetic values of the literati came to dominate the garden art of the Wei and Jin Dynasties.

Sui and Tang: A Period of Prosperity

Fig. 16 The famous Wangchuan Valley *by Anonymous (Song Dynasty). The original was created by Wang Wei centuries before.*

The first centuries of renewed imperial rule in China saw a pattern of unity and division. In neither case did the political environment make much difference to the educated class. After rule by two emperors in the Sui Dynasty (581–618) came the Tang Dynasty (618–907). Built on the Sui's secure foundations, China entered into a period of unprecedented unity and prosperity. The Tang government built up the imperial examination system to re-engage the intellectuals in support of the state. They were now given opportunities to rise to top positions in government, to become wealthy overnight, creating legends of "rags to riches" success. Nevertheless, the risks of a political life were considerable and difficult to predict, which laid more psychological pressure on the arrivistes. As a result, they saw gardens as their own self-contained world, where they could relieve tension and feelings of stress or anxiety.

Such a historical context gave great impetus to the development of the scholar's garden, which gradually developed its own unique style. Of all the scholar's gardens of that period, the best known was perhaps Bai Juyi's. Bai dedicated poems and essays to his own private garden at Lüdaofang in Luoyang in central China's Henan Province. His poems bring to life the relationship between intellectuals and their gardens, a living testimony to the saying, "A man is known by his garden." Gardens, according to Bai, are not only

places filled with flowers, grasses, and picturesque landscapes, but also faithful mirrors of real life. An arrangement of elements within a garden such as he described became the reference point by which all subsequent gardens were judged.

The villa garden, as its name suggests, evolved from earlier houses and gardens, where their function had gradually shifted from agricultural production to recreation. Although these gardens had varying names and sizes, they came to represent a comfortable life in a peaceful countryside. Wang Wei (699–761), a mid-Tang painter-poet, restored a famous villa and garden at Wangchuan (Rim Valley). The forty poems he wrote of his work at Wangchun, and the *Sketch of Wangchuan* (Fig. 16), a long painted scroll he made of the garden, preserved its memory through the following centuries.

Some modern scholars argue that traditional China featured a dual system of government: the imperial family and a massive civil service. But in reality the civil service system, to some extent, became the dominant element within the structure. Intellectuals-turned-officials held effective power and certainly had a powerful influence on their locality. One well-known official, the poet Bai Juyi, when he was governor in Hangzhou, ordered the construction of a new dam to the West Lake, and greatly enhanced the landscape by planting trees around the lake, restoring riverbanks, and building new tourist attractions. Bai Di, or the Bai Juyi Causeway, was named after him, and is still one of the most visited sites in Hangzhou today. Bai Juyi not only devoted himself to landscape gardening, but also left behind numerous poems and essays that shed light on issues of theoretical significance. No wonder he is considered the very first scholar-gardener in China's history, or the pioneer of the classical Chinese garden concept.

In traditional China, there were no open public spaces. Even markets were contained within walled enclosures. As a result, Buddhist and Taoist temples became major public places frequented by city residents. The monks and priests would hold temple fairs or public festivities; and many Chinese literati, who saw the study of Buddhism as both an intellectual and a social activity, would meet friends, compose and recite poems, and enjoy flowers in bloom and the full moon in the temple gardens.

This cultural context helped turn the temple gardens into holy sites in harmony with more worldly tastes. Solemn but not depressing, large but not overbearing, these temple gardens closely followed the style of the scholar's garden. In Chang'an, capital of the Tang Dynasty, temples and monasteries could be found everywhere, some as large as an entire city block. Most temples had gardens within their grounds, creating a different atmosphere from that of the other city spaces, an ambience of benign nature essential to religious sites.

By the time of the Tang Dynasty practical gardening skills had developed and a wider range of plants were grown. Exotic flowers and blooming trees filled each temple garden. Some temples eventually became famous for their unique flowers. Located in Xi'an, northwest China's Shaanxi Province, the Ci'en Temple was best known for its peonies and lotus flowers, a great public attraction for the local people and the literati alike. The arcane art of plant hybridization had developed to such a high degree, and peonies, expertly cultivated, could now be found with flowers in many refined hues and shades (Fig. 17). In addition to evergreens like pines and junipers, flowering trees were also grown in Buddhist temples, which, according to Bai Juyi's poems, were expected to help visitors understand the most profound Buddhist tenet: "form itself is emptiness; emptiness itself is form."

By contrast, Taoists believed that the magic peach was a fruit that enabled people to live longer, and that explains why so many peach trees are to be found in Taoist temples. The glorious peach blossoms, in turn, helped bring fame to many Taoist sites. Not only did Taoist temples flourish in great numbers in cities, they were also dotted around the outskirts and in the open country. Almost every scenic spot in China features religious architecture, which not only brings a touch of culture to the setting, but offers comfortable accommodation to visitors as well (Fig. 18). More importantly, the natural environment of China helps to create the otherworldly atmosphere of a religious sanctuary. By the end of the Tang Dynasty, the pattern in which Buddhism and Taoism dominated their respective sacred mountains had substantially taken shape and has remained the same until today, although the religious buildings themselves have experienced many changes.

However, it is the royal garden that best reflects the majesty and grandeur of the golden age of Tang, the unprecedented period of prosperity of the unified power. Tang followed the example of Sui in adopting the two-capital system. Accordingly, imperial palace gardens were constructed in both Chang'an and Luoyang. The imperial garden styles had by then become highly diversified, with well-defined and quite specific functions and usages: the imperial garden within the capital city, the garden outside the capital city, and the garden for short stays away from the capital.

The Daming Palace, for example, was where the Tang emperors lived for most of the year. Although not the central palace, Daming was by no means less important than Taiji Palace (the Supreme Palace), the official imperial residence. A self-contained palace city on the eastern outskirts of Chang'an, Daming was divided into three major parts: the Palace Court (Fig. 19), the Eastern Inner Garden, and the Garden District. Next to the Daming Palace was a huge

Fig. 17 Peonies "Grand Beauty" *by Ma Yi (Qing Dynasty).*

遠公晉遠池種白蓮以千

白社之中陶調明謝

一因無酒而不至一好

長未對淵從靜云淵

少林元度謝山亂吉逐来

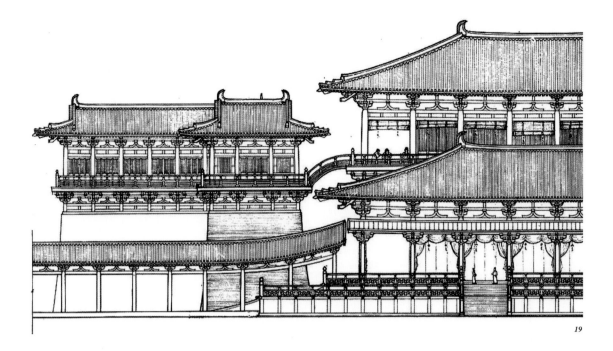

imperial park, heavily forested with only a few buildings visible. The park functioned, among other uses, as a farm to supply the imperial court with fruit, vegetables, poultry, and fish.

The severe climate in Chang'an, particularly the summer heat, led the emperors to construct a number of imperial summer resorts. The famous Western Garden of the Sui Dynasty, among others, was second in size only to the Shanglin Yuan (Imperial Forest Garden) of the Han Dynasty, an artificial mountain and water garden. Inside the Western Garden, sixteen separate enclosed precincts were grouped around an artificial lake named the North Sea. Longlin Canal wound past the front gate of each precinct before finally joining the North Sea. Moreover, five lakes were excavated south of the North Sea, each with an artificial island in the middle, and lavishly embellished with gorgeous buildings to symbolize the supreme power of the emperor and the vastness of the empire.

The Tang, besides taking over royal gardens from the Sui, had quite a number of new palaces constructed. Famous for its hot springs, the Huaqing Palace was first built as early as the days of Shi Huangdi, first emperor of Qin, used by Emperor Wu of Han (141–87 B.C.), and expanded in the third year of the Sui Emperor Wendi's reign (581–604). During the reign of Emperor Taizong of Tang (627–649), Huaqing Palace was further enlarged, with its architectural layout remodeled after that of Chang'an. Among the best known hot springs were the Nine Dragons Spa (where emperors bathed with their concubines), Guifei Spa (exclusively reserved for the Imperial Consort Yang Guifei, one of the most romantic figures of Chinese history) (Fig. 20), the Morning Star Spa, and the Prince's Spa.

The Tang emperors were surnamed Li and claimed Lao Tsu, the philosopher, as their ancestor, for Lao

Tsu, according to tradition, was also surnamed Li. Consequently, they respected and advocated Taoism. In most cases, Taoist temples were found in the imperial gardens—some were Taoist temples in a real sense while others were essentially ornamental, serving only to add variety. The imperial gardens of this period were created primarily as a symbol of grandeur and power rather than to express feelings and good taste; yet that power was waning inexorably.

Fig. 18 Viewing the Lotus on Lu Mountain, *from the series* Famous Chinese Figures and Their Stories *by Shangguan Zhou (Ming Dynasty). It was very fashionable at that time for literati to discuss Buddhist scriptures with monks.*

Fig. 19 Section plan and interior of Linde Hall of the Daming Palace (Tang Dynasty).

Fig. 20 Emerging from the Huaqing Pool *by Kang Tao (Qing Dynasty) depicts the imperial concubine Yang after bathing.*

20

Northern and Southern Song Dynasties: A Turning Point

To the north and west of the Great Wall of China was a vast population of nomadic peoples—Mongols, Jürchen (the ancestors of the Manchu Qing Dynasty), and numerous other tribes. Already the Jin and Liao tribes had moved south of the wall and set up kingdoms. It was these northern peoples who confronted the Northern Song Dynasty (960–1127) when it conquered northern China in the 10th century, and it was their growing power that forced the Song (960–1279) to abandon the north and their capital Kaifeng, and withdraw to south of the Yangtze River in 1127, becoming the Southern Song Dynasty (1127–1279), with their capital at Hangzhou.

Eventually, in 1279, the Southern Song fell before the power of the Mongol confederacy, with Kublai Khan establishing the Yuan Dynasty (1206–1368) and eventually reuniting the whole of China. Some modern scholars suggest that the best era in which to have lived in history was during the Song Dynasty, simply because it is one of the few dynasties in China's history when no civil officials were killed for political reasons. The Song Dynasty has been politically underrated because it only exercised sovereignty over a part of the country and suffered from an endemic military weakness. However, as far as the educated were concerned, it was indeed one of the best dynasties. In general, the Song Dynasty was relatively benign: a less rigid rule and more freedom of speech. Both science and technology made great advances, and most of the Four Great Inventions of which the Chinese

people are proud (the compass, papermaking, gunpowder, and printing) took shape during this period. Important books were produced like *The Treatise on Architectural Methods* by Li Jie, and the *Timberwork Manual* by Yu Hao.

Hailed as the pinnacle of Chinese artistic achievements, the fully developed Song culture began to steer away from what previous cultures had embraced. As the interior world of the Song scholars became more intensely focused, they turned their attention from the outside world to probe their inner worlds of emotions and feelings. Their aspiration for real mountains and water was then transformed into a desire for idealized artificial landscapes (Fig. 21). The Confucian slogan—"Those who excel in literature are entitled to pursue a political career"—helped bring large numbers of outstanding men of letters to the fore in the bureaucratic stratum. Even Emperor Huizong of Song himself was a highly accomplished painter-calligrapher (Figs. 22–23).

The literati gave a powerful impetus to the development of art of the garden and transformed it, gradually, into a system of intellectual meaning and effective communication. Both the ideal content and the best form of the garden were now being settled and thereby becoming idealized models for later generations to follow.

Landscape painting of the Song Dynasty reached the zenith of style and sophistication. Almost all of the Song landscape paintings were embellished with

21

architectural details as a means of incorporating cultural elements into a natural landscape (Fig. 24). Architecture had become central to the Chinese aesthetic of landscape. It gave structure to nature, and virtually created a place to be visited, to be viewed, and indeed, to be experienced. Here was a concept usable at all levels in garden design to "artificialize" (and improve) a natural landscape. Quite a number of paintings from the Song Dynasty depict gardens in a variety of different ways: in full, in part, in detail, or simply portraits of the life lived in the gardens. These images provided a secure aesthetic foundation for the literati who wanted to know how to manage their gardens. Painterly concepts were infused into actual landscaping, so that gardens became three-dimensional landscape paintings.

A garden became a place where the Song men of letters could enjoy their rich social and creative lives. In addition to the four traditional arts (lute-playing, chess, calligraphy, and painting), sampling tea, observing flowers and plants, collecting antiques, and Zen practice and meditation had all become an integral part of life. This spiritual world constituted major factors to be considered in garden design. To associate themselves more closely with their gardens, scholars directed their feelings and aesthetic sense toward flowers, birds, fish, and insects as much as into mountains, waters, trees, and rocks. Consequently, the Song Dynasty saw an extraordinary flourishing of garden building: imperial palaces, private houses, government offices, monasteries, public places, and even teahouses and wine shops had gardens to attract visitors.

The best-known garden of the Northern Song Dynasty was the Gen Yue (also known as the Hua Yang

Palace), which was the imperial garden of Emperor Huizong (1100–1125). The garden was designed, in part, by the emperor himself. Huge efforts were expended to make it a microcosm of the natural world. Great quantities of fine stone were imported to make mountainous rock gardens from which water would cascade, drip, or slowly seep—a miraculous mélange of sound, sight, and smell. With its pools nestling among the hills and streams circling the mountains, the Gen Yue reminds us of the strong relationship between mountains and water in traditional Chinese aesthetics. Yet it existed all too briefly. Less than four years after the Gen Yue was completed, the Eastern Capital (Kaifeng) was captured by the troops of the Jin Dynasty (1115–1234). Snow and icy winter storms led thousands of citizens to swarm into the garden and tear down all the buildings for firewood, marking the tragic end of a miracle of garden art. Also remarkable was the Jinming Pool, in what is now Henan province. This was another imperial garden that became well-known for the popular sport of dragon-boat racing in later years. This huge pool was roughly square in shape, with a bridge linking the southern shore to the domed Shuixin Hall in the middle, built on a cross-shaped terrace (Fig. 25). Most royal gardens of the Song Dynasty were regularly open to the public, a rare practice in dynastic China.

In the period of the Northern Song, private gardens were at their best in the Central Plain and south of the Yellow River. In his *Record of Famous Gardens of Luoyang*, Li Gefei, a renowned Northern Song scholar, documented as many as nineteen gardens of note, including three flower gardens, six domestic gardens, and ten villa gardens. Also worthy of note is the Garden for Self-Indulgence once owned by Sima Guang (1019–1086), a Northern Song historian, so named because Sima believed he could neither have empathy with the broad masses of the people (like the great sages), nor live an austere and impoverished life like the wise men of former times. All he could

Fig. 22 The Auspicious Cranes *by Zhao Ji (Song Dynasty).*

Fig. 23 Cottonrose Hibiscus and Ornamental Fowl *by Zhao Ji (Song Dynasty). The artist Zhao Zi is better known as the renowned aesthete, Emperor Huizong of Song.*

Fig. 24 Four Landscapes *by Liu Songnian (Song Dynasty). The principal characteristic of Song Dynasty paintings is simplicity and elegance. These paintings directly influenced the gardens.*

24

Fig. 25 **To Win the First Prize in Jingming Pool** *by Zhang Zeduan (Song Dynasty). Jingming Pool was an imperial water garden, also used for naval maneuvers.*

do was to improve his own life and find joy in following his own path, because this was the truest reflection of his desires and beliefs. Most of the buildings within Sima's garden were named by him after the hermit sages in history, thereby claiming a connection through allusion to the life and work of celebrated scholars.

The Southern Song chose Lin'an (now Hangzhou) as its capital, moving their political center to South China. As a result, economy and culture south of the Yangtze River were energized, and Song patronage produced a new boom in the creation of gardens. Imperial gardens in Lin'an centered on the West Lake, but they were fairly small in size because of the declining power and wealth of the Song rulers. After the Jin armies captured the Eastern Capital of the Northern Song, they looted the cultural relics and forced the Han scholars to move to the Middle Capital (now Beijing). In today's Beijing, architectural relics from the Jin Dynasty can still be found: the magnificent rock gardens in the Gen Yue Imperial Garden were moved to the Qiong Hua Island in Beihai (North Sea) Park.

To express the extraordinary beauty of Suzhou and Hangzhou, local people often quote an old Chinese saying: "Above there is heaven, and below there are Suzhou and Hangzhou." Both cities were easily accessible by land and by water, and were famous for their traditional handicrafts. When the Song Dynasty came

to power, Suzhou and Hangzhou were at their apogee, with numerous gardens that were already famous. Among the few that have survived is Canglang Pavilion, or the Surging Waves Pavilion in Suzhou.

First built by Su Shunqin (1008–1048), a well-known writer who lived in Suzhou for three years, the pavilion has a clear pond sandwiched between two green bamboo groves, creating a sense of seclusion and privacy, and adding dramatic shadow and light to the surrounding architecture—an ideal place to enjoy moonlight and a cool breeze. Built around a unique network of waterways, Suzhou is exceptionally suitable for gardens. Many traces of gardens left by the Song Dynasty can still be found today, providing at least a general picture of the landscape patterns and water systems. Private gardens also abounded in Hangzhou, although only a few dozen of them were documented in the historical record. One of the most notable was Meng Creek (Dream Creek), owned by Shen Kuo (1030–1095), author of *Writings Beside the Meng Creek*. It is said that he once dreamed of a beguiling landscape garden when he was thirty years old. Thereafter, that vision haunted his dreams until one day he found precisely the garden of his dreams in Runzhou, offered for sale by a Taoist priest. Convinced that it was a gift from heaven, he bought and transformed the garden into his home.

By the end of the Northern Song Dynasty, a marked difference in garden style existed between the north

and the south. While the gardens in North China were larger in size, featuring both hills made of packed earth and natural landscapes, those in the south seemed to be more the product of design and artifice, filled with highly prized stones carved by the natural forces of water and wind, and with exquisite pavilions and other architectural highlights. As time went on, the southern style gained the upper hand and shaped the garden development path for the Ming and Qing Dynasties.

However, the scholar's gardens of the Song featured a simple, expansive, elegant, and natural style, a living embodiment of the aesthetic tastes of the literati. Simple design meant better results with less effort, and a fuller expression of individual feelings without the overuse of technical devices. But the essence of these gardens was a kind of imaginative boundlessness, where the mind and spirit could roam unfettered. They denote a preference for the ideal over the real, for fantasy over fact, just like large areas of blank space left in traditional Chinese paintings. Elegant design suggests more attention is paid to such refined artistic elements such as pines, plums, and bamboos.

The Northern Song poet Lin Hejing (967–1028), for example, was known for his literary name, Plum Wife and Crane Children: he was so detached from the worldly concerns that he seemed to have plums as his wife and cranes as his children (Fig. 26). Finally, natural design means a preference for a touch of the wild, with emphasis both on harmony with the natural landscapes outside the garden, and a proper balance between flowers, trees, and architecture inside. Typical of the paintings created by the literati, these features

are what set the Song private gardens apart from those of the Ming and Qing Dynasties.

The Southern Song saw a remarkable development of Buddhism. As a symbol of local Buddhism, the Zen was the most powerful in the Southern Song, and it was during this period that the famous "Five Mountains and Ten Monasteries" were built. The establishment of the complete seven-structured temple compound system (Shichido Garan) marked the complete Sinicization of the Buddhist architectural style and a remarkable turn toward secularism. While Karesansui (dry landscape gardens, also known as waterless gardens), a typical Chinese Zen garden style, disappeared in China, it gained popularity in Japan and has endured there ever since (Fig. 27).

The flourishing of Buddhism not only gave birth to monastery gardens, but also led to the building of monasteries within natural landscapes. Of the various ancient sites that have survived, those that feature monasteries were mostly established during the Song Dynasty. Monastery buildings would, in one way or another, draw people to them. One example is the West Lake in Hangzhou: there, apart from the natural beauty of the landscape, the Buddhist temples around the lake also played a vital role in shaping the environment of the area. Accordingly, West Lake became one of most famous public gardens, known far and wide in the Southern Song Dynasty for its "Ten Spectacular Views."

Fig. 26 Crane Playing on Gu Mountain, *from the series* Famous Chinese Figures and Their Stories *by Shangguan Zhou (Ming Dynasty). Traditionally cranes were thought to represent high-mindedness, a quality that the literati attributed to themselves.*

Fig. 27 The Shi Garden of Longan Temple in Japan. These dry gardens derived from Chinese "withered landscapes." They were inspired by Zen thinking and are commonly called "Zen gardens" in the West.

Yuan, Ming, and Qing
Dynasties: The Last of the Best

Most ancient gardens we see today were created during the Ming (1368–1644) and the Qing (1616–1911) Dynasties, although those from the latter account for a larger number. Intact gardens from the Ming era are indeed few and far between, but partly preserved architectural structures of that period are more common. Masterpieces from the Ming and Qing Dynasties are the swan song of the garden art of dynastic China—all the techniques and craftsmanship were at their best and had reached their fullest maturity. Meanwhile, the natural elements revealed in the paintings of the Northern and Southern Song Dynasties were steadily declining.

The Yuan (1206–1368) originated in Mongolia and the Qing in Manchuria: only the Ming was an authentically Han Chinese dynasty. The Yuan and Qing both adopted many aspects of Han culture and society. Nevertheless, they retained their own customs, social structure, and even language. Both became thoroughly Sinified, and China absorbed much from their new rulers. The Yuan rulers chose Dadu (Great Capital, now Beijing) as their capital city and built gardens on the former sites of the *yuanyou* of the Liao (907–1125) and Jin (1115–1234) Dynasties. Most royal gardens were located in the imperial city, centered around Lake Taiye (now Three Seas, in Beihai

Park). But Yuan rule lasted less than a century.

The Ming and Qing marked the peak of absolute monarchy in dynastic China. As set out in the Ming legal codes, all the land and people of the entire empire belonged to the emperor. No individual had the freedom to decline to serve as an official. If a person refused to be appointed as an official by the emperor, he might as well be put to death. With an all-powerful neo-Confucianism dominating society, any independence of expression by the scholars and literati was curtailed and their intellectual independence lost. All of these negative outcomes were attributed to the formidable rule of the rigid feudal system. Gardens, as a result, became the last free spiritual home of the scholars.

The structures and architecture in any Ming or Qing gardens create the effect of a courtyard, with an axial symmetry and a sharp distinction between hierarchical levels, a reflection of the omnipresent Confucian ideology. The garden itself, however, was an exception in that there were no rigid axial lines or hard and fast directions. Instead, a garden could offer a flexible space for fine rocks, water, trees, pavilions, corridors, etc., creating a space defined sensually rather than mathematically (Fig. 28). This landscape, not surprisingly, became the last spiritual refuge for

the literati. Therefore, the scholar's gardens, with those of the Yangtze Delta as the prime examples, became the paragon of classical Chinese garden art.

To create a profound artistic conception within a narrow space, it is essential to employ all possible techniques to enhance the feeling of space and heighten the contours and fine details. In this period, the skills of rock placement, the design of water features, the cultivation of flowers and trees, and the installation of architectural ornaments all achieved unprecedented heights of creativity (Fig. 29). Most notably, plants were treated with exceptional care. So, the branches of pine and plum trees, in particular, were trained into picturesque shapes to frame a view. These measures, together with the sophisticated techniques of borrowed landscape and contrasting scenery, were used in almost all private gardens of the Ming and Qing Dynasties.

These garden views were the most carefully and painstakingly prepared man-made achievements (Fig. 30), and yet evoking the air and sensations of mountains and woods was actually the most sought-after effect. Seen in a positive perspective, the landscaping skills in question had achieved a significant level of sophistication, developed entirely through creativity and innovation. But from a negative perspective, the views were unnatural, created out of a somewhat sterile aesthetic preoccupation.

Since the Song Dynasty, the growing prosperity of urban commerce had brought about a thriving civil culture. Unlike the traditional scholar's gardens of the previous dynasties, those of the Ming and Qing became worldlier, incorporating more elements of popular culture. Garden architects now ranged from the intelligentsia and officialdom at the top level down to out-of-favor scholars, craftsmen, and merchants on the lower rungs of society, and this wide range added depth and dimension to garden art. Therefore, different aesthetic interests found their respective expression in the gardens of the Ming and Qing, and this variety determined the essential features of garden design.

Ming rulers lived deep within the palace, and seldom walked beyond the city walls. As a result, they only concerned themselves with the Three Seas inside the imperial city and the imperial gardens within the Forbidden City. Nevertheless, private gardens of this period were well-developed, with those of Beijing as the paramount examples. Among the monographs on landscape gardening, *Treatise on Superfluous Things* and *The Crafts of Gardens* are of special note. Five of the twelve volumes of the *Treatise—Houses and Dwellings, Flowers and Trees, Waters and Rocks, Fowl and Fish,* and *Vegetables and Fruits*—are directly related to landscape gardening, while the remaining five volumes such as *Calligraphy and Painting* and *Ornamental Tools* are indirectly related. One of the most classic works in the history of Chinese garden making, *The Crafts of Gardens* summarizes and elaborates the technical specifications and aesthetic principles for gardens on the Yangtze Delta, covering

29

such topics as location selection, construction, land-scaping, and plant choice.

The book was produced at the end of the Ming Dynasty by Ji Cheng, a famous late-Ming garden architect. Ji Cheng shifted his attention to landscape art following a career failure, when he was incriminated because the author of the book's foreword rebelled against the Ming Dynasty. Interestingly, the book then appeared in Japan and was hailed as the classic theoretical monograph on world landscape gardening. It was not until the era of the Republic of China (1912–1949) that the book again caught the attention of Chinese scholars.

The rulers of the Qing Dynasty came from the barbarian lands beyond the Shanhaiguan Pass on the Great Wall. After they took power in China, they preferred to live in gardens and open spaces; the planning and site selection of the city of Beijing speaks volumes about their inclination to live near water and grass. It is extremely rare to have pools and lakes located right in the middle of a city in China, and Qing emperors built imperial gardens on the outskirts of the city as their summer residences. Emperor Kangxi (1661–1722) ordered the construction of The Garden of Everlasting Spring (Changchun Garden) on the northwestern outskirts of Beijing and Chengde Imperial Summer Resort (about 140 miles northwest of the capital) and these became models for palace gardens away from the Forbidden City. Typically, the Qing emperors would live in their garden palaces for most of the year, governing China from a place of repose. The Forbidden City was used only for ceremonies and celebrations, and it was only on major holidays and for special occasions that the emperors would return to their principal imperial palace.

After Emperor Yong Zheng succeeded to the throne in 1722, he expanded the Old Summer Palace bestowed upon him into an official palace garden complex. Henceforth, five successive emperors after him all lived and handled state affairs there. Repeated extensions and refurbishments had created a very functional family residence. Over a span of more than 130 years, it developed into one of the most important palaces of the mid-Qing era, and the *de facto* political center of China.

When Emperor Qianlong (1735–1795) came to power in 1735 (Fig. 31), a period of peace, an economic boom, and his penchant for grandiose projects led to the third wave of intense garden construction, following in the footsteps of the Qin and Han, as well as those of the Sui and Tang Dynasties. The most notable gardens include the Three Hills and Five Gardens in the northwestern suburbs of Beijing. "Three Hills" refer to Jade Spring Hill (Garden of Tranquility and Brightness), Fragrant Hill (Garden of Tranquility and Pleasure), and Longevity Hill (Garden of Clear Ripples). "Five Gardens" are the Old Summer Palace

Fig. 30 The southwest corner of the Garden of Cultivation, a landscape of trees and rocks in miniature. Such exquisite gardens are normal in Suzhou.

Fig. 31 Emperor Qianlong of Qing Viewing the Painting by Lang Shining (Qing Dynasty). Even emperors sometimes wanted to withdraw from the cares of office.

and four adjacent gardens: Eternal Spring, Blossoming Spring, Warm Spring (predecessor of Qinghua University), and Bright Spring, which together formed a massive network of gardens on the outskirts of the capital. Simultaneously, the Imperial Summer Resort outside the Shanghaiguan Pass was also further expanded to form one of the largest imperial gardens.

In the mid and late periods of the Qing Dynasty, China became more closely linked with the Western world. In the 18th century, Chinese gardens were held in great esteem in Europe and had a profound influence on European garden making. Meanwhile, in China gardens were also being influenced, in part, by the Western world. When glass came to late Qing China, it was widely used in private gardens. Influenced by the Western style, quite a few of them had stained glass installed to create a dreamlike effect. Western elements were most prominent in merchants' gardens, primarily for reasons of ostentation. Within the Lion Grove Garden at Suzhou, the architectural style of the small bridges, even that of some small buildings, was obviously Western. However, the main structures still retained the traditional Chinese style.

As the imperial capital, Beijing had numerous private and palace gardens in its own unique style, which were as good as, if not better than, their counterparts in South China. Additionally, gardens south of the Five Ridges in southwest China developed into a distinctive private garden style, just as famous as those in North China and south of the Yangtze River. Together they constitute the three major types of private gardens.

The 1860s, the declining years of the Qing Dynasty, were perhaps the worst in Chinese history, and certainly the most destructive time for gardens. The rapacious foreign powers wreaked unprecedented havoc on both imperial gardens in Beijing and private gardens of South China. As domestic troubles trod upon the heels of foreign invasions, China's feudal society was breathing its last. Predictably, the ancient art of garden making was plunged into an almost terminal crisis.

The Qing Dynasty finally came to an inglorious end in 1911, but the old lifestyle that had both created and sustained traditional gardens had already waned. The social stratum of literati and intellectuals who had invested their energies in garden making faded away, leaving behind nothing but a physical (and slowly decaying) outer form. Only after the foundation of the People's Republic of China in 1949 was the process of loss and destruction arrested. The majority of the remaining classical gardens were nationalized, with a program of renovations carried out to restore their

original structure, with the gardens then being opened to the public as national parks. On the one hand, this change has had some impact on the original garden culture, originally designed for the pleasure of the elite few; on the other, it also enables more people to tour and visit these gardens, thereby coming into contact with and enjoying this cultural heritage.

In recent years, since China's economy began its sustained spurt of development, and the country opened increasingly to the outside world, China's gardens have begun something of a renaissance. As the Chinese people have started to take a second look at their traditional culture, gardens are beginning to receive more and more attention. This cultural heritage has also exerted a positive influence on today's construction. Quite a number of well-known gardens have been listed as world cultural heritage sites by UNESCO.

Classical Chinese gardens are revealing their unique charm in the new era. As the outside world has rediscovered the quality and richness of Chinese gardens, many of which have miraculously survived the turmoil of the 19th and 20th centuries, more and more visitors are coming to China for the unique experience of its traditional culture, in these gardens with their millennial history and sublime beauty (Figs. 32–34).

AESTHETICS AND LANDSCAPING

Gardens represented a bridge between man and nature, a concept that ultimately became a common feature in gardens globally. Often a garden's structure and organization suggested an ideal, inflected by an individual's perception of the world and subtly exemplifying the relationship between man and nature. Classical Chinese gardens strongly reflected these dualities. They were suffused with the worship of nature implicit in traditional Chinese culture. Rocks, lakes, flowers, and trees were all personified or endowed with spiritual meanings.

The Aesthetic Schemata

*Fig. 35 One aspect of the
Erfen Bright Moon Building
in Yangzhou.*

In many cultures the garden makes a clear statement about aesthetic identity. This is certainly true of China where reverence for nature—high mountains, deep valleys, great lakes, and mighty rivers—has always been part and parcel of traditional culture. This view of the natural world has inspired the Chinese people to think more coherently about life, as evidenced by the Confucian doctrine that one should polish oneself like jade. In this system of values, human beings view themselves as part of the natural order, and thus nature becomes a crucial element in their aesthetic

35

perceptions, which impinges directly on every aspect of daily life (Fig. 35).

The traditional Chinese aesthetic has been built upon absorbing a great variety of ideas and tastes. This openness makes it possible to embrace cultural elements from many sources, a quality that has been considered one of the positive features of the Chinese approach to the world. It draws inspiration from the exuberance, richness, and abundance of nature, and from this raw material, forms new cultural and aesthetic concepts. Not all of these ideas manifest fully in China, but sometimes they do so elsewhere. For example, dry landscape gardens originated in China, but only really thrived in Japan. This is because the Japanese, an island people, needed to combine beauty with their limited range of natural resources, and so, reshaped what was originally a Chinese concept. In China itself by contrast, the objective has always been to aim for inclusivity in an aesthetic experience, taking and including all that nature offers, the more the better. Thus, a Chinese garden contains a multitude of expressive moments achieved through a near infinity of interwoven perceptions and connections.

Historically, China has been a huge and central-ized empire, and its aesthetic value system has been shaped both by that physical scale, and by its cultural and spiritual depth. From a negative standpoint, this omnivorous urge to embrace and include everything is one of the weaknesses of traditional Chinese culture: abundance creates confusion and incoherence. Yet a more positive view suggests that this bold pursuit of inclusivity succeeds more often than it fails, by some means constructing unity out of disparity. In the world of gardens, one example of this mysterious process of creating integrity out of what might oth-erwise be mere random elements is the aptly-named Garden of Perfection and Brightness. This imperial park built by Qing Emperor Yongzheng long before his coronation is also called the Garden of Gardens and includes almost all of the best features of gardens of every style within its boundaries (Fig. 36).

This inclusivity, of course, carries a political message. Making their garden a microcosm of the Qing Empire's infinite variety and bringing order out of what might otherwise have been an aesthetic chaos speaks volumes about the emperors' ambitions. They wished to exercise the same strenuous efforts to bring harmony through power, control, and careful management to the entire Chinese macrocosm. In the microcosm of a garden a large space with nothing in it is merely emptiness, while a disorderly multitude of plants and other objects leads only to an unappealing muddle. At the macro-level of the Chinese people, "middle" and "central" are two key concepts, as revealed by the name "China" (Middle Kingdom) itself. They were equally significant in Chinese gardens.

Fig. 36 Orchids by the Lake depicts one of the Forty Sights of the Garden of Perfection and Brightness, personally chosen by Emperor Qianlong to be celebrated in paintings and in verse.

Something in the middle of an area epitomizes power and prestige, and central locations are closely associated with beauty. These two standards work well for the traditional Chinese built environment. Chinese architecture emphasizes horizontal compositions, creating little, if any, sense of vertical movement. Therefore, in most cases, a group of individual buildings is integrated into a whole horizontally, and the relationships between buildings are best defined by their proximity to central positions.

Landscaping art in China emphasizes a perfect combination of the unusual and the traditional, conforming to the all-encompassing pursuits inherent in Chinese culture. Traditional Chinese gardens are supposedly an epitome of the freestyle design. Unlike formal, geometric European gardens, axis, symmetry, and hierarchy do not seem to prevail in China, as if no rules existed. In fact, landscaping activities in dynastic China were controlled by the established aesthetic principles of the Chinese people. Between "unusual" and "traditional," the latter is more important. Strict conformity to feudal rites, rituals, central axes, and a hierarchy of location was essential for private gardens in South China, let alone in Beijing, the capital city. Careful observation and interpretation will help to identify the impact of "central" and "traditional" doctrines on the artistic tastes manifested in Chinese gardens.

To create a garden, the first step is to choose a location and setting, and then mark the center point. Spatially speaking, the main scenic area with such major landscaping elements as architectural structures should be placed in the middle and have control over

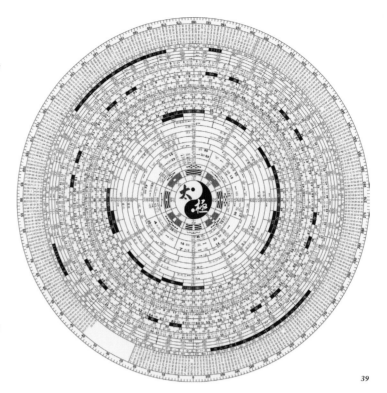

39

subsidiary areas around the center. What's more, the "traditional" principle manifests itself in the maxim that most significant structures within the main scenic area face due south. Governed by such constraints, Chinese gardens remain essentially the same despite all apparent changes, with the "unusual" maxim less powerful than the "traditional," as illustrated by what Confucius said, "Do as you like, without violating the rule" (Figs. 37–38).

Chinese gardens are associated with literary writings and landscape paintings. Theoretically, they share the same fundamental rules, including the primary-secondary relationship. Like a painting, the most significant landscapes in a garden should face the viewer, although less important ones can be either hidden or visible. And this, accordingly, determines the main direction or "tradition" of a garden, the absence of which would invariably turn a feeling of wholeness into a sense of disorder.

Obviously, feng shui (Chinese geomancy), once a system of positioning physical objects in environmental locations, has made a profound impact on the aesthetic value system of the Chinese people. Located in the northern hemisphere, most of China's territory lies in areas between the temperate and subtropical climate zones. Topographically, it is high in the northwest and low in the southeast, with major rivers running eastward into the sea. The southeast wind prevails in summer and the northwest wind in winter, and as such, it goes without saying that all houses should face south so as to take in more sunshine in summer and resist cold wind from the north in winter. Combined with the traditional Chinese principles

Fig. 37 Parts of the Erfen Bright Moon Building in Yangzhou. Although all buildings are rectangular, there is still variety in form and impact.

Fig. 38 The point of entry to a garden prepares a visitor for all that follows within.

Fig. 39 A compass, the essential tool for a geomancer to position a building.

Fig. 40 Flowing water is a symbol of life. Its impact enhances the sound and sight created by falling water.

41

Fig. 41 The "mountain top" of Jichang Garden in Wuxi leaves the visitor with a powerful sense of untamed nature.

Fig. 42 Rugged yellow stones in the Zengzhao Garden in Changshu contrast effectively with the water.

of *yin* and *yang*, *wuxing* (five elements), *bagua* (eight diagrams), *jiugong* (nine palaces), as well as astronomical and mathematical science, they form a complicated and all-encompassing theory, defining a rather mystical, one-to-one relationship between geographical location, architectural form, and luck.

Chinese geomancy, after all, is the traditional art of successfully orienting buildings. When designing and siting buildings, geomancers would use a *luopan* (compass) (Fig. 39) to determine the most favorable location for buildings so that the forces of *yin* and *yang* were balanced correctly, thereby reducing the chance of illness. The Chinese aesthetic schemata established over the centuries led most Chinese architectural structures to be domestic rather than institutional (Fig. 40) and with emphasis on the security provided by a walled enclosure.

According to Chinese geomancy, a garden should be relatively closed to the outside world, which would help create a self-contained environment or the so-called "Sky in a Pot" free from external disturbances and distractions. Walls, therefore, have played a key role in garden design, where height, texture, and degree of openness can be easily adjusted to meet such traditional aesthetics as constructing the big picture from small details, and a changing view with each step one takes.

Chinese gardens, in essence, manifest a paradoxical sort of artificial naturalness, as best evidenced by the "scholarized" landscaping art developed from the culture of the literati and scholar officials. This unique artistic style comes from nature, but it was thought superior to nature. As the last spiritual home to the literati, gardens have become an idealized "artificial-natural" space where contradictions between Confucianism and Taoism, freedom and ritual, dream and reality, and academia and officialdom all glide into a unified whole (Figs. 41–42).

Landscaping Elements

Architecture

Rock Stacking

Waterscapes

Plants

Borders

Scenic Route

Fig. 43 The roof line of the booth in the middle of Dianchunyi Courtyard of the Wangshi Garden in Suzhou contrasts with the surrounding walls.

Fig. 44 View of the Island Hill of the Humble Administrator's Garden in Suzhou. The building, the rocks, and the expert use of plants create a perfect visual harmony.

All of the elements then available were used in Chinese classic gardens to make living sights (Fig. 43). In addition to the key elements such as architecture, stone, water, and plants, the master designers also used animals, sounds, seasons, and changes between dawn and twilight as well as quotations from poems and essays. A comprehensive perspective is needed to appreciate Chinese gardens (Fig. 44), which are

difficult to construe literally. Meanwhile the wear and tear from age tends to wipe out the living or invisible elements, leaving the engineering parts. The maintenance of gardens needs the same skills required to build them. A brief view of the landscape is just a clue to what is there, and the best way to appreciate the gardens is to go there repeatedly at different times.

43

Architecture

- *Tingtang*
- *Xuan*
- *Xie*
- *Ting*
- *Louge*
- Boat Hall
- *Shi*
- *Langzi*
- Bridge
- Ornamental Windows
- Furnishings

Fig. 45 The exterior yard of Ancestoral Hall in the Lion Grove Garden. The open passage between the atrium and the living rooms is on a grand scale, and the configuration of the courtyard is symmetrical. Plants and flowers add atmosphere.

Fig. 46 The Little Fish Pavilion of the Garden of Cultivation survives from the Ming Dynasty. Its style is more constrained than that of the Qing Dynasty.

In general, buildings take up some 20 to 30 percent of space in a typical Chinese garden, more than any other landscaping element. Traditionally, a garden embodies the concept of the "oneness of man and nature" (Fig. 45). One of the key elements of garden landscaping, the architectural structures symbolize mankind or the activities of mankind. Since architecture is a major part of landscape, its forms and styles are supposed to meet more stringent aesthetic standards than other elements (Fig. 46), although the composition

of architectural styles and the relationship between individual structures are quite flexible.

Chinese culture attaches great importance to the naming of things, and as such, name and object often bear a thought-provoking relationship. Different architectural names signify different forms and functions, and suggest their specified locations within the garden grounds. More importantly, a wide variety of architectural forms and styles will add interest and value to garden landscapes.

Tingtang

A *tingtang*—similar to a "hall" in English—functions as a major architectural element in Chinese gardens. In fact, a *tingtang* is a compound of *ting* and *tang*, the former being the place to discuss affairs, and the latter referring to a bright, sunny, and large room. Since their functions tend to overlap, they are collectively termed *tingtang*.

As clearly stated in *The Crafts of Gardens*, the first step in any garden design is to locate the *tingtang*, the main visual element and the setting for dinner parties and social gatherings. In most cases, a *tingtang* is situated right in the middle of the most significant and largest scenic area, a reflection of the traditional view, "what is central is more important."

As the most public space in a garden, a *tingtang* is often lavishly decorated, its style and furnishings usually determining the aesthetic character of a garden.

Among the various architectural forms of a *tingtang*, twin-hall, a typical building in South China, is worthy of special note. Facing in opposite directions with their backs to each other, the south hall is used to keep warm in cold winters, and the north one to provide shade in hot summers. When a twin-hall opens on four sides, it is called a four-sided hall.

In most cases, a *tingtang* stands above its surrounding area. Accordingly, it requires large space around so as to serve the purpose of public use, maintain the proportional relationship between architectural size and environment, and conform to the traditional Chinese view that outdoor activities are more important than indoor entertainment. Although there may be several *tingtang* in a large garden, one will be the most massive and magnificent, with the most lavishly decorated rooftop.

47

49

Xuan

In South China, a *xuan* is the courtyard in front of a building. As an architectural style, it normally refers to a building open on three sides. Sometimes, a *xuan* performs the same function as a *tingtang* when there is no *tingtang* in a garden. Historically, numerous buildings were called *xuan*, as this type of architecture provides a better view of the outside world. To maintain the corresponding relationship between architecture and landscape, most *xuan*, as the name itself suggests, are located in areas of open space.

In general, a *xuan* is flexible in size. However, be it large or small, it is not supposed to be bigger than a *tingtang*, nor smaller than a chamber or studio. Sometimes, a *xuan* is joined together with a covered walkway, either placed in the middle or at the ends. When no window frames are installed, it actually resembles a pavilion.

Fig. 51 The small With Whom Shall I Sit? Pavilion in the Humble Administrator's Garden; the building's name is a playful commentary on solitude. Its design is unusual, based on a fan motif. The floor plan is fan shaped, and the unusual window and a fan inset in the ceiling pick up the theme.

Fig. 52 The Listen to the Rain Room in the Humble Administrator's Garden in Suzhou. Here one can listen to the rain fall on lotus and banana leaves, as described by the Song poet Yang Wanli.

Fig. 53 The Xiao Cang Lang of
the Humble Administrator's
Garden has a dual function. It
is both a waterside pavilion to
watch the water on both sides
but also a gallery bridge, below
which the fish can swim.

Fig. 54 The Breeze House in
the Lingering Garden, Suzhou.
The curved back of the Meiren
kao—a type of bench seat—was
designed so that women (and
indeed, men) could lean out
and watch the fish in the water
below. The latticed window
in the side wall provides an
additional "borrowed view."

Xie

In ancient times, a *xie* denoted a building that stood
on a high terrace, or a waterside structure in a garden,
hence the name *shuixie*, or water terrace. Almost
all Chinese gardens are filled with water features,
although the areas of water bodies differ from each
other in size. Consequently, the *xie* has always been
one of the most popular architectural forms in gardens. The side of a *xie* that faces water usually offers an
open view from behind the rails, which alludes to the
image of a beautiful woman sitting still in meditation.
While relaxing at the water's edge, visitors can delight
in feeding fish or chatting with friends.

In a private garden, a *xie* is usually not very large,
because its size must comply with that of the body
of water. By contrast, the size of a *xie* in an imperial
garden must be large enough to match expansive
water views.

Ting

Fig. 55 The Crane Booth of Xia Mountain of the Geyuan Garden in Yangzhou. The upswept outer tips of the eaves might suggest a flying bird's wing.

Fig. 56 The splendid double-layered six-sided booth of the Yuyuan Garden in Shanghai accentuates the peaks of the surrounding rock garden.

Literally, a *ting* is a sheltered place to stop for a rest, equivalent to the English word "pavilion." As one of the simplest architectural elements with a wide variety of styles, pavilions are found not only in gardens but in other public places as well. A tree, a rock, and a pavilion, when expertly combined, may serve as the landmark of any traditional Chinese garden. Architecturally, Chinese pavilions are the same as those in European gardens, but since most of the latter are built of stone or masonry and seem more massive, their styles are considerably different.

In a Chinese garden, pavilions are usually the place to get the best view of the surrounding area. With many sizes and styles, pavilions can be located almost anywhere, even on the summit of artificial hills to become attractions in their own right. More interestingly, their roofs come in many different shapes and forms: round, square, hexagonal, octagonal, triangular, diamond, half-hidden behind walls, single-tiered, or double-tiered.

In terms of function, pavilions fall into three major categories: a *nuanting*, or sun pavilion (with windows); a *beiting*, or stele pavilion (lined with steles); and a *jingting*, or well pavilion (with a well dug inside). What is unique about a *jingting* is that the middle of its roof must be open so as to facilitate communication between man and heaven. As a special architectural element of Chinese gardens, most *jingting*, not surprisingly, are built beside libraries, alchemical furnaces, or ancestral halls.

55

Fig. 57 The Laojun Hall of the Yuyuan Garden in Shanghai has a unique composition, with double-layered booths in front of the double-layered pavilions.

Louge

A *lou* refers to a two-or-more-story building, and *ge* is a tall building with an open-sided ground floor. In most cases, however, they are used interchangeably, and collectively called *louge*.

Louge are usually built along the perimeter of a garden to relieve the sense of isolation created by substantial walls. In addition, *louge* may come in a wide variety of forms to serve an equally wide variety of functions without producing any sense of oppressiveness.

Ge are often located in fairly large gardens to become part of the scenery and, more importantly, to add vertical movement to the horizontal line of architectural structures. Since *louge* are seldom built in the middle of Chinese gardens, they do not demand space in this key area. Equally, very few pagodas, another type of tall building constructed for religious purposes, can be found in private gardens, although there are quite a number of them in imperial parks.

Boat Hall

An interesting architectural form, boat halls refer to boatlike structures perched at water's edge. In South China, it is considered great fun to go boating on rivers or lakes. A fisherman, according to traditional Chinese culture, is often closely associated with a hermit, and therefore boats have become iconographical symbols for the reclusive life.

What is interesting about boat halls is that, unlike ordinary architectural structures with sides longer than the main facades, they point their shorter sides to the lake center, creating a feeling as if they were about to sail off into the blue.

While some boat halls look exactly like boats berthed on water, some others seem more like *shuixie* (water terraces) than boats, only suggestive of boats at the water's edge, with a rectangular body and cabin windows. Still others look like something between these two examples, with *xuan* in the front, a *shuixie* in the middle, and a small *ge* at the back. Quite a number of boat halls, surprisingly, are located far from water and technically called "boats on land," a unique architectural form mainly used to express one's desire for a secluded life.

58

Fig. 58 The Land Boat Hall of Yuyuan Garden, Shanghai is well placed in the landscape.

Fig. 59 The "boat without a mooring" of Guyi Garden, Shanghai. The prow of the boat is shaped like the summit of Xie Mountain.

071

Aesthetics and Landscaping

59

Fig. 60 The Ouyuan Garden, Suzhou. A Qing Dynasty garden with areas to the east and west of the main house. Here, buildings are small and intimate, suggesting a private space.

Fig. 61 Within the Five Ancient Pines Court in the Lion Grove Garden. The garden is renowned for its flamboyant decorative woodcarving within the main buildings. Here, the decorative motif of the doors is huge and features exotic leaves.

Shi

As part of a building, a *shi* refers to a closed, private room, mostly serving as the study or bedchamber, where distinctive interior designs tend to reflect the aesthetic taste and inner world of the garden owners. Usually located in the innermost parts of a garden, and enclosed by lines of courtyards, most *shi* are small and in the peaceful setting of a secluded courtyard. Unlike the large halls and terraces in the open area, they strive for elegance and delicacy, with the expectation that they will reveal the ideals and ambitions of their occupants.

Langzi

One of the most commonly used landscaping elements, a *langzi*, more often known as a "covered walkway" or "corridor," is an important part of the scenic route that leads visitors through a garden. *Langzi* can come in straight or curved styles, running up the hill or across the lake, forming an enclosed courtyard or linking major delightful sites together. Master landscapers use expertly designed twists, turns, and rises and falls to determine the best sequence of views. One of the finest examples would be the *langzi* up the hill of the Lingering Garden, which swirls abruptly just before it reaches the summit, leaving visitors to marvel at the intriguing view of the *langzi* itself.

Sometimes a partition wall is placed in the middle of the walkway to turn it into a double-lane *langzi*, where latticed windows are usually installed to make landscapes on both sides visible, and thus enabling visitors to enjoy dramatically varied views as well as creating the illusion of larger space. Among the less common categories of the *langzi* found in huge gardens with tall buildings, are those installed with sunny windows and called a *nuanlang* (warm walkway), and those with upper and lower stories are termed "double-deckers." Double-deckers are few and far between in private gardens.

Fig. 62 *The north corridor of the Heart-Ease Study of the North Sea. Its wall is the outside wall of the garden.*

Fig. 63 *The double-sided corridor of the Yiyuan Garden in Suzhou.*

Fig. 64 *The ascending corridor of the Zhanyuan Garden in Nanjing is like a mountain path, rising and falling.*

Fig. 65 The long zigzag bridge of Yuyuan Garden, Shanghai, under which shoals of carp swim back and forth.

Fig. 66 The small stone bridge of the Wangshi Garden is simple but decorated by a stylized peony deeply carved on the highest step.

Bridge

While a body of water signifies separation with a hint of mystery, a bridge symbolizes connection with a thrill of expectation. In traditional Chinese gardens, the bridge is viewed as an exceptionally poetic landscaping element whose presence never fails to suggest the quest for the unknown.

In large gardens, man-made bridges come in a wide variety of unique forms and styles, offering potent additions to the surrounding landscapes. In most cases, arches are used in long-span bridge structures to reduce the load and improve structural efficiency. The jade belt, one of the unique types of Chinese bridges, features round arches and thereby forms a complete circle with its own reflection in the lake. The curved bridge is usually built immediately above the water to make visitors feel as if they were walking on the lake. Other notable types of bridges include the simple masonry vault between two peaks, the rustic wooden footpath, the covered bridge, and the pavilion bridge, found over large lakes. A good example of the last category would be the Five-Pavilion Bridge on the Slim West Lake in Yangzhou.

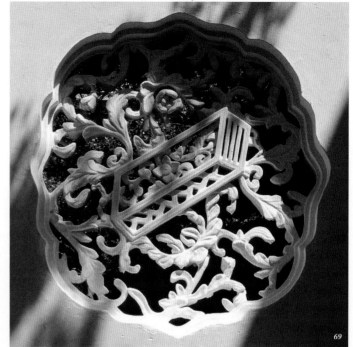

Ornamental Windows

Garden architecture is an art that emphasizes fine
details. Whether installed in walls or elsewhere,
ornamental windows come in a variety of shapes and
styles. In South China, landscapers pay particular
attention to the close match between window patterns
and the landscaped plants, and go to great lengths to
make the window lattices blend in well with the shape
of the twigs and branches around them.

*Fig. 67 A view into "another
world" from the western
half booth in the Humble
Administrator's Garden in
Suzhou. The circular doorway
focuses on the vista like a
camera lens.*

*Figs. 68–71 Chinese gardens use
all sorts of beautiful windows,
apertures, and delicate grilles to
allow the spectator an enticing
glimpse through the wall into
the garden beyond.*

Figs. 72–74 Door frames
determine how views are seen.

Fig. 75 Beautiful windows of
Heyuan Garden in Yangzhou.
From the inside of the building
the shapes of the windows frame
the view; seen from the outside
the windows break up a blank
expanse of wall.

Furnishings

Fig. 76 The stone lion of Xuyuan Garden in Nanjing.

Fig. 77 The elegant interior and furniture of the Celestial Hall of Five Peaks of the Lingering Garden in Suzhou.

Fig. 78 The composition of the Xuyuan Garden in Nanjing. The lakeside rocks, the "mountain peaks," the cobbled pavements made in flower form as well as the stone tables and chairs make a satisfying harmony.

Fig. 79 Interior view of the Hall of Drifting Fragrance of the Humble Administrator's Garden in Suzhou.

Apart from the landscaping elements discussed earlier, furnishings and decorative items carefully placed in the rooms and chambers of a garden also play an important role in adding the depth of beauty of an interior space—stone tables and chairs, strangely shaped rocks, potted landscapes, paintings, and calligraphy by ancient artists, etc. Regrettably, however, the passage of time and events have left few ancient gardens exactly as they were in their heyday. Historians and researchers sometimes have to dig deep into the archives to re-create the rich details in question.

78

79

Rock Stacking

⊙ **Hillside** ⊙ *Fengluan* ⊙ **Valley** ⊙ **Bonsai**
⊙ **Cliff** ⊙ **Cave** ⊙ **Path**

Fig. 80 The Cloud-Capped Peak of the Lingering Garden in Suzhou. It is on a gigantic scale, and with many complex stone forms, immensely impressive.

Fig. 81 A charming vignette of children at play in the Autumn Hall by Chen Zongxun (Song Dynasty).

Fig. 82 One corner of the Winter Mountain of Geyuan Garden in Yangzhou. The view of bamboo through the aperture works well with the white stones on the other side of the white wall: "snow-capped peaks" and spring foliage.

Artificial hills (Fig. 80) are considered the creative works of art that make Chinese gardens unique. Understandably, the size of artificial hills in the gardens of South China is not on a par with that of the real mountains in some of the imperial parks. Lishan Mausoleum built by Shi Huangdi, for example, is in every way a masterpiece, with trees and grasses carefully planted on top to look exactly like a real mountain. The trend to build huge mountains continued well into the Han, Wei, Jin, Southern, and Northern Dynasties.

Starting with the Tang Dynasty, landscapers began to build small hills resembling huge mountains in shape, but not in size (Fig. 81), and thereby marking the beginning of the second stage in the art of rock stacking. Since the hills thus created were similar to landscape paintings or bonsai, they gradually became the mainstream of rock stacking in later dynasties.

When it came to the Qing Dynasty, such architectural style met with criticism from scholars, thus heralding the third stage in the art of rock stacking: to model an artificial hill after a part, not the whole, of a real mountain in a reduced scale, or to create a lifelike image of a well-known vista. Most of the hills

81

thus created were built of earth, interspersed with rocks, and heavily forested, leaving visitors to feel as if towering peaks, steep cliffs, and rolling hills were close to the garden walls.

Although developing sequentially over time, the succeeding stages did not replace the earlier forms. Each style had its enthusiasts, and so they overlapped, came back from being unfashionable, and even intertwined. In later years, the artificial hills, particularly those rock gardens built entirely of stones, became substantially the same as architectural structures except for different appearances and building materials, and as such they greatly enhanced the feeling of space and added to the scenic appeal.

Building materials for rock gardens include small-sized, egg-shaped lakebed stone, large, cube-shaped yellow stone, and blue slabs from North China, ideal for spectacular landscapes. Among these three categories, lakebed stone from South China is the most valuable, because its texture and composition look very much like the brushstrokes of a Chinese painting, which explains why some ancient literati were ardent rock collectors (Fig. 82).

The development of freehand painting techniques improved the literati's uncanny ability to embrace both the beautiful and the ugly. In fact, ugly objects stand a better chance of breaking away from traditional constraints, and thereby become more desirable works of art with their powerful impact and unusual aesthetic appeal. Interestingly, the lakebed stone is not completely natural. After chiseling holes into the stone, the ancient artisan, according to tradition, would sink it into the lakebed and let time wash away his marks. Many years later, when the stone was finally brought up from the lake, it became, once again, a "wonderful gift from nature." Since lakebed stones have uniquely irregular shapes, it is virtually impossible to fit them together by size, shape, color, and texture. Architecturally, a typical rock garden is composed of various landscape elements.

Hillside

Rocks are scattered along the gentle slope to resemble the side of a mountain, as seemingly commonplace as they are metaphorically profound.

Cliff

As clearly stated in *The Crafts of Gardens*, the cliff is a hill built against a wall. Thoughtfully created cliffs feature a variety of forms and styles: some steep, some overhanging, some perching on the water's edge, some shadowboxing with their own reflections on the lake, some resembling a landscape painting produced on a canvaslike wall, and some looking like a three-dimensional picture with a framed image of pines, bamboos, and plums.

Fig. 86 *The Autumn Mountain of Geyuan Garden in Yangzhou, where yellow stones covered with lichen catch the evening sun.*

Figs. 87–88 *One part of the towering rock garden of the Huanxiu Mountain Villa in Suzhou.*

87

88

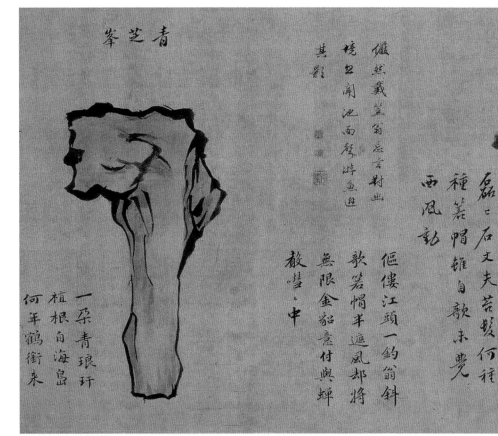

初三月依約眉
痕一搦多
廑何時移珮環長廊
散花女

箬帽峯

儼然戴笠翁此言對出
燒虹闌池西發將魚遊
其影

磊磊石文夫苦髮何種
種箬帽雄自歌未覺
西風起

傴僂江頭一釣翁斜
欹箬帽半遮風却將
無限金韜意付興蝉
散髮中

青芝峯

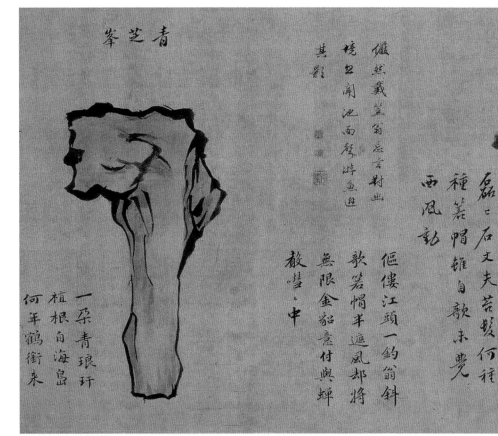

一朵青琅玕
植根自海島
何年鶴衔來

攙槍昌清風事
庭遺清風入錦鶴

仙掌峯

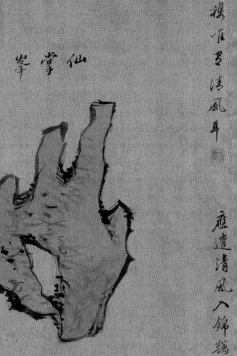

曾向米海嶽題匾九曜石
如何掌上看任有蘚花碧
西彼有仙峯
扶雲出寫掌
池上妙蓮開
因之勃遐想

苔蘚重作錦致不冰泷
露只拿雲滾散捏得如椽
筆慈鞍羊欣白練裙
廊有三石刻

千霄峯

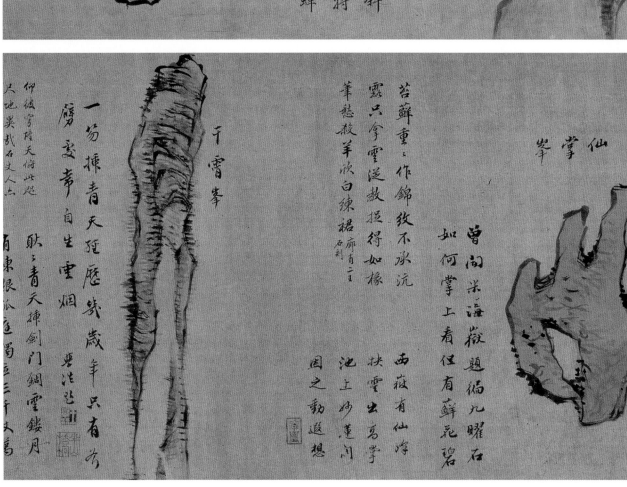

一笱揰青天狂歷幾歲年只有青
劈愛帝自生雲煙
耿耿青天揰劍門鎖雲鏤月
仰彼穹陰天倚此起
大地奚我石丈人乎
有東浪沁逢昌立三千又萬

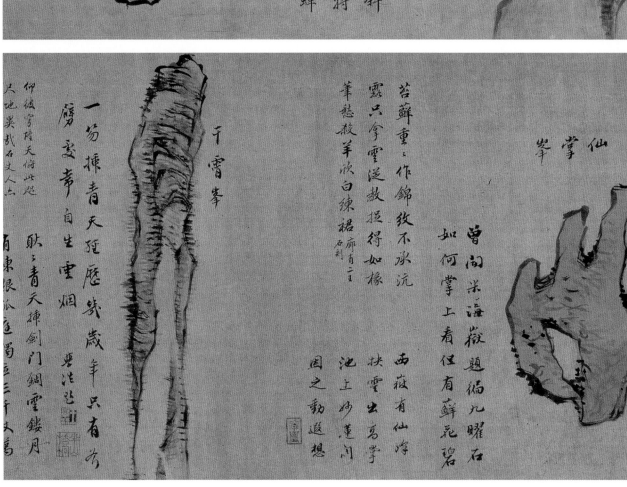

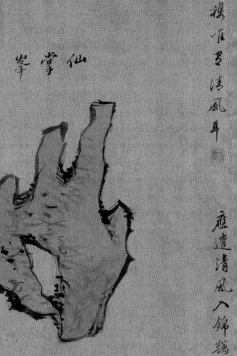

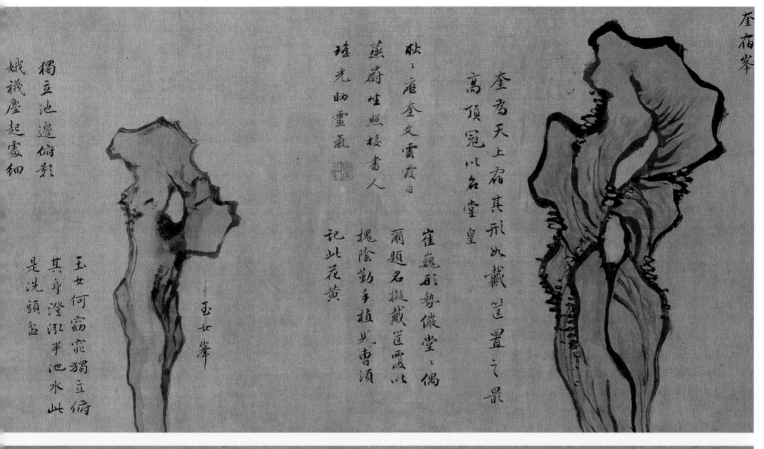

奎宿峯

奎為天上宿　其形以戴筐置之景

高頂冠以名堂皇

昔　唐奎文雲霞曰

崔巍形勢儗堂〻偶

蘭題名擬戴筐霞以

藜蔚笙照校書人

槐陰勤手植此曹須

雄光助靈氣

記此花黃

玉女峯

獨立池邊俯影

娥裳塵起霧細

玉女何竛竮獨立俯

其身澄泓羊池水此

是洗頭盆

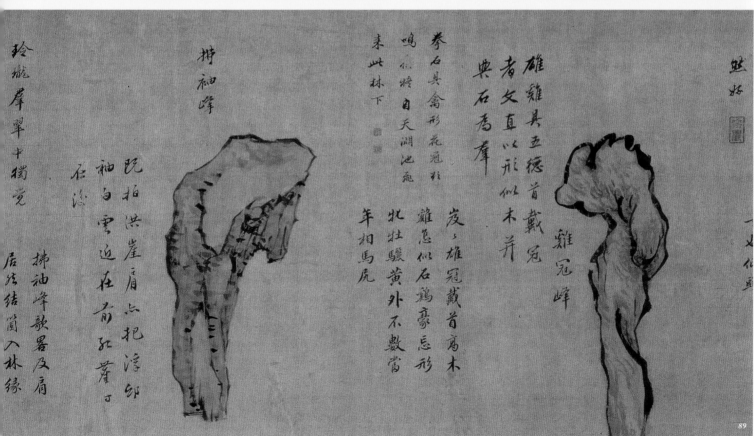

雞冠峯

雄雞具五德首戴冠

者文直以形似木并

典石為摹

拳石具禽形花冠形

雞怎似石鷄豪忘形

鳴〻將目天湖池氣

北牡驪黃外不數當

年相馬兕

朱此林下

袱袖峯

玲瓏群翠十擱覺

居坐結閒入林緣

玩拍洪崖肩忘把淨邙

袖句雲迫在前孔萼

在溪

拂袖峯歌暑及肩

093

Aesthetics and Landscaping

89

Fig. 89 This finely worked drawing catalogs the different types
and categories of ornamental
stones used in gardens. Some
of the shapes were especially
prized and immensely valuable.

Fengluan

A compound of a *feng* (towering peak) and a *luan* (rolling hill), *fengluan* in most cases are modeled after real mountains in South China. Some others follow the style of the Stone Forest in Yunnan province. Still others are huge boulders that stand alone as symbols of peaks. To successfully accentuate their height and grandeur, it is inadvisable to grow any plants on peaks or hilltops.

Figs. 90–93 A collection of rocks evocative of mountain peaks.

Fig. 94 The "mountain ranges" of Zhanyuan Garden in Nanjing.

94

Cave

As a curiosity, a few mysterious caves house tunnels that run through mountains. Some others are just cells where visitors may stop for a rest. Still others are half-filled with water to enhance the air of isolation.

Fig. 95 The man-made caves of Xia Mountain in the Geyuan Garden at Yangzhou.

Fig. 96 Within the stone structure of Autumn Mountain of Geyuan Garden in Yangzhou. Light floods into the cave.

Valley

Valleys without streams flowing through them are named "dry valleys"; those with streams are more accurately called gullies, where the height difference creates waterfalls.

Path

Most staircases running uphill are paved with stone slabs, aiming to achieve the feeling of walking on a winding trail.

Fig. 98 The steep rocky steps of Autumn Mountain of Geyuan Garden in Yangzhou rise up through magnificent acers.

98

Bonsai

Fine rocks placed into bonsai pots add beauty and charm to any picturesque setting, especially small courtyards.

Waterscapes

- Pond
- Stream
- Gully
- Fountain
- Lake
- River
- Pool
- Boulders

Fig. 101 Tongli in Suzhou. Water is an indispensable element for a garden.

Fig. 102 Lotus, duckweed, and carp are basic materials in a classical Chinese garden design.

Fig. 103 The waterfalls of the Lion Grove in Suzhou cascade down a narrow gully.

Water is the soul of all gardens (Fig. 101). It has many different roles and functions. It reflects the sky, moon, flowers, trees, and architectural structures to create a feeling of heightened space (Fig. 102). It provides the habitat for aquatic plants like the lotus and a home for fish. The sound of water—cascading, running, trickling, and dripping—creates an ambience. On large pools you can even idle in a boat on the surface of the water. Ancient Chinese gardens, in fact, are characterized by extensive use of water features, as documented in such literary sources as *The Book of Poetry*.

As most of the gardens in South China are fairly small, it is necessary for landscapers to use water features to create special effects so as to achieve expansive water views. Basically, there are two spatial relationships between water and rock. On the one hand, the rock features may be located at the end of a pond to face the principal building from a distance, in a vertical direction to the water surface; on the other hand, they can be placed parallel to each other to create intimacy and a sense of romance.

Architecturally, living water from the river source is fundamental to a fine garden. Except for the limpid water in a pool (to create a sense of seclusion), all other waterscapes must be traceable to their sources. More often than not, the origin of a stream is hidden deep in a grotto, which becomes a curiosity in its own right.

Garden architects often use special water management techniques to create dramatic water areas and shape their boundaries (Fig. 103). Balanced, well-designed shorelines are expected to match the architectural style of a garden. Natural shorelines come in two types: stone and mud. Stony shorelines decorated with rocks are more popular, but muddy ones give a real sense of wildness. Generally speaking, the height difference between the shore and the water surface should be kept small enough to maintain an intimate relationship between man and water.

Pond

A rectangle or any other shape, filled with still water, and without islands, bridges, or very rugged shorelines.

Fig. 104 *The still waters before the Erfen Bright Moon Building in Yangzhou reflect a mirror image of the buildings.*

Fig. 105 *The Zuibai Pool in the Songjiang District of Shanghai. The platform juts out into the water, allowing the visitor a closer view of the fish and the water plants below.*

Lake

Either large or small with rugged shorelines and coves,
dotted with bridges, islets, and rockeries.

Fig. 106 Waterscape of the Lingering Garden in Suzhou.

Fig. 107 Waterscape of the Guyi Garden in Shanghai. The largest body of water is always
the core area of the garden, and the most important buildings are positioned around it.
The shoreline is dramatic and full of changes through the seasons.

Fig. 108 Waterscape of Zhanyuan Garden in Nanjing under a covering of snow. The winter
vista is considered as important as those of spring, summer, and autumn.

106

107

Flowing into a lake or winding its way through a garden.

Fig. 109 A stream with floating lotus leaves in the garden. Lotus growing unconstrained can easily fill any body of water. The best plantings keep it under control, so the water can still be seen.

River

Longer and wider than a stream.

Gully

Sandwiched between two hills, filled with running water, and different from a valley in that it features waterscapes while a valley offers mountain views.

Figs. 112–113 Stones, water, moss, and lichen: the essential interaction produced by nature.

Pool

Small, deep, blue body of water that adds great interest and charm to a peaceful setting when placed immediately below a waterfall.

Fig. 114 Deep dark pools are enlivened by brightly colored fish.

114

Fountain

Featuring cheerful and bubbling movement of water, or an artificial pool beneath a rockery resembling a natural fountain with water falling down from the crevices when it rains.

Boulders

Dotted on water's surface or sandy shores, one of the most commonly seen water features.

116

117

Plants

Fig. 118 The Yuyuan Garden in Shanghai. Carefully color-graded azaleas provide a seasonal set piece.

Fig. 119 Despite colorful blossoms, it is the freshness of the bamboo foliage against the white wall that is the essence of spring here.

Fig. 120 The Humble Administrator's Garden in Suzhou. Airy spring blossoms contrast with wintery leaves of bamboo. Slim plants are chosen to highlight the expressive force of the lines in small spaces.

Fig. 121 Plants' arrangement in Yuyuan Garden in Shanghai: thick flowers and leaves have made a wonderland.

Fig. 122 A hot pink azalea highlights the feathery new foliage of the moundlike acer. Its lightness is accentuated by the huge paddlelike bright green leaves of the banana to the left.

As one of the most essential landscaping elements, plants bring the essence of nature to gardens, symbolizing life, vitality, and growth (Fig. 118). To create a painterly setting, landscapers need years of disciplined training and professional experience to select the right plant for the right place. The arts of propagation, hybridization, pruning, and shaping are really the preserve of the specialist gardener. Plants provide the elements of change in a garden through the seasons, but they are also the most demanding element in terms of labor, care, and management (Fig. 119).

Traditionally, a person's taste in plants has long been used as a clue to his character or traits. The chrysanthemum, for example, symbolizes a longing for a reclusive life; the lotus epitomizes purity; the knotty bamboo suggests noble character and integrity; the plum in snow is considered an emblem of endurance; the pine signifies longevity and immortality; the orchid is associated with innocence and culture; and the peony is hailed as the queen of all flowers. Most of the ancient garden owners turned to plants as a means to express their feelings (Fig. 120).

More importantly, plants help create a sense of increased space by partitioning the garden into sections and creating depth, shadow, and light with their canopy. Chinese gardeners, however, will neither use geometrically pruned plants nor wall-like fences. Instead, they tend to seek more natural means to adjust visual effects. In South China, where the mild climate is ideal for plants, many different species are available (Fig. 121). In the cold North China, by contrast, evergreens are probably the best for winter landscapes.

In Chinese gardens where the architecture emphasized horizontal direction more than vertical movement, the landscape was basically defined by its plants. In addition, carefully laid out plants added visual interest and charm to otherwise dull landscapes with their rectangular and square-shaped buildings.

Aesthetically, Chinese culture attaches great importance to the physical form of plants. The gardeners tend to go so far as to twist the tree trunks or prune them into a manageable form. Accordingly, the garden architects prefer to use gracefully flexible trees like camphor and elm. Of special interest is the Chinese weeping willow with long flexible twigs, which is often planted at the water's edge because its massive canopy does not make a good specimen for a small courtyard.

In addition to visual effects, the Chinese architects pay serious attention to the acoustic effects produced by plants (Fig. 122). It is not uncommon for them to manipulate trees to achieve the desired sound effects— the rain dripping on to the huge leaves of banana trees and lotus flowers, and the wind sighing through the pine woods. In fact, the chirping of birds and cicadas also has a lot to do with plants. Equally important, the seasonality of plants is something a good gardener knows well. As the flowers bloom and fade, and the leaves turn red and yellow, spectators are filled with anticipation for a wide array of different landscapes in the different seasons. If properly maintained, different varieties of garden flowers will bloom in succession for up to nine or ten months a year, and thereby provide a visitor with different aesthetic experiences (Figs. 123–127).

121

122

Figs. 123–127 *The bright flowers*
of Campsis radicans *billow over*
a solemn green Parthenocissus.
In autumn the roles are reversed
as the plainer vine colors
change to dramatic scarlets and
crimsons.

Borders

- ⊙ Wall
- ⊙ Walkway
- ⊙ Water
- ⊙ Artificial Hill
- ⊙ Pavement

Fig. 128 Structures, walls, water, and stony banks make up the multiple boundaries of the garden.

Fig. 129 The boundary between the rocks and the boat hall of the Yuyuan Garden, Shanghai: white stone walls, rooflines, and the land boat.

Fig. 130 The second door of the Garden of Cultivation in Suzhou, with a cobbled path simply planted on each side leads to the smooth stone floors of the main scenic area. The hard landscaping underfoot is handled with consummate expertise in Chinese gardens.

Architecturally, the garden boundaries can be defined in various ways to achieve better visual effects (Fig. 128). The classical Chinese garden, be it large or small, always consists of several scenic areas of different sizes, which are in turn further divided by circuitous walkways, flower-walls, and buildings into small courtyards displaying different themes. Since the traditional Chinese landscaping arts place a strong emphasis on the "borrowed view," the concept of boundary refers not only to the geographical demarcation line itself, but to the farthest points of the visible space (Figs. 129–130).

Wall

Fig. 131 A diagrammatic sectional view of the Stone Forest in the Lingering Garden in Suzhou, where the space is divided by walls, and the spaces linked by the stone paving underfoot.

Fig. 132 The dragon head at the end of the Cloud Wall of the Yuyuan Garden, Shanghai.

Fig. 133 The pattern of vine stems, and the shadows they create on the white wall are an important year-round feature, independent of foliage or flower.

One of the most physical means for marking the end of a garden, the outer wall is usually tall and imposing to keep out unwanted people. However, the walls within a garden are mainly used as partitions to separate courtyards and scenic areas. The architects prefer to install decorative windows and loop-holes on the wall for "borrowed views." Sometimes, bamboo fences are erected to substitute for a wall.

Among the various types of garden walls, the most notable are the whitewashed wall topped with black tile, the rolling cloud wall, and the winding dragon wall. Sometimes, ancient vines and exotic rock gardens are placed at the foot of these walls to create the effect of a traditional Chinese watercolor painting.

132

Fig. 134 Seemingly natural-looking outcrops of rock combined with natural green foliage are characteristic of the Huanxiu Mountain Villa of Suzhou.

Artificial Hill

Typical artificial hills fall into three major categories: earth, stone, and stony earth. A hill built entirely of earth features an extensive, gentle slope, and a natural look, whose defining effects are less strong than the other two, and therefore it is seldom used in small or medium-sized gardens.

Usually fashioned after natural hills, artificial hills lined with stones and caves form part of the winding scenic route, marking the borderline in a more delight-ful and meaningful manner.

Hills of stony earth come in a wide variety of land-scape forms, offering an ever-changing view of the garden as the visitors walk along the footpaths. More importantly, the viewpoints on top of the hills overlook the whole garden and bring the scenery beyond the garden wall into view, creating a feeling of larger space.

Fig. 135 The steeply ascending
covered corridor in the Beihai
Park is like a path up a
mountain.

Fig. 136 A section of the Water
Corridor of the Humble
Administrator's Garden in
Suzhou.

Fig. 137 The water corridor to the
Building of Reflection in Water
of the Humble Administrator's
Garden in Suzhou confidently
zigzags, rising and falling, in
front of the With Whom Shall I
Sit? Pavilion across the water of
the pool.

129

Aesthetics and Landscaping

Walkway

In most cases, the walkways in a garden are placed close
to the wall. The enclosures of various sizes between
walkways and walls are usually adorned with small
plants, ornamental rocks, and miniature landscapes to
add color and interest to the otherwise dull landscape
resulting from the straight and level wall.

Sometimes the walkway runs through the
garden, drawing an imperceptible line between two
waterscapes at a level just above the water surface.
When seeing the view on both sides, the spectators
feel as if they are walking on water.

Pavement

One of the easiest ways to define the border of garden space is to use pavements of different materials and colors. The pavement for water terraces, for example, is usually of stone blocks carefully laid out by rubbing the adjoining surfaces until they fit together. For the passages, walkways, and hill paths, brick, slab, and pebble are used to protect the pavement against the ingress of rainwater and from erosion of wind and rain.

Fig. 138 Different surfaces for different effects in the Humble Administrator's Garden in Suzhou. The bridge is paved on horizontal strips while the pathways are cobbled.

Figs. 139–140 The paths are made up of small cobbled stone, inset with different colored stones in a regular motif. Here this diminishes the monotony of a long straight pathway.

Fig. 141 The Wangs' Yard in Yangzhou. Each side of the round doorway is paved with different materials, indicating a demarcation between the two spaces. The identical stepping stones on each side provide a visual link.

Water

As a perfect boundary marker, the water surface itself offers a strong sense of space. Since the uninterrupted space above water does not block views, waterside gardens are expected to make the best use of this feature.

The Surging Waves Pavilion, among others, is a typical waterside courtyard with a stream running west to east in front of its southern gate. The stone bridge spanning the water enables tourists to enjoy the courtyard view even before they enter the gate. The winding corridor that follows the terrain of the mountain connects water and architecture together, creating perfect "borrowed views" with their latticed windows, where there is no division between interior and exterior, and no feeling of inside and outside. This open space technique has helped make the Surging Waves Pavilion a famous public garden over the years.

Almost all of the private gardens around the West Lake are free of walls on their water-facing sides,

including the Liu Village, Guo Village, and Jiang Village. By using the winding shores of the lake as a suggestion of garden boundaries, the natural lakescape beyond the courtyard is entirely integrated within the garden.

When the Summer Palace in Beijing was constructed, the architects paid great attention to the combination of the garden with its surrounding landscapes. The outer wall at the southwest corner, for example, is sufficiently far away from the center so as not to block the view of the natural landscapes around the Jade Spring Hills. Viewed from the Front Hill and the lake center, the outer wall seems nonexistent. A large expanse of fields beyond the lake in the south seems connected with the landscapes in the garden simply because the whole area south of the Seventeen-Arch Bridge is free of walls, separated from the water surface outside the garden with causeways only.

Fig. 142 Waterways outside the Surging Waves Pavilion in Suzhou is intended as a boundary and to expose the scenery.

Fig. 143 The Mountain Villa Guo in Hangzhou is next to the West Lake, and the water becomes a natural boundary.

Fig. 144 The complex waterscape in front of the Breeze Pool Hall and the Western Building of the Lingering Garden in Suzhou. The water flows below the building to the right, which provides a comfortable viewing platform; the fine rocks on which it is supported connect visually to the rock display alongside it.

Scenic Route

- ◉ Corridor
- ◉ Intersection
- ◉ Rock Garden
- ◉ Waterway

Fig. 145 The Lingering Garden, Suzhou. The roofed corridor controls and defines the route for vistas of the garden, setting up a series of carefully chosen vistas for the vistor.

Fig. 146 The screen before the Garden of Cultivation, which visually separates the inside world from the outside. Entering a garden should come as a surprise.

The main scenic route in a garden leads visitors through many points of interest, like a guided tour (Fig. 145). To make the best use of a limited space, the route is often located close to the outer wall. Sometimes pavilions and terraces are erected to provide elevated viewing platforms for visitors to overlook the garden view (Fig. 146).

As most classical Chinese gardens were built and owned by scholars, cultural elements have exerted a great impact on garden designs. Numerous inscribed couplets and plaques highlighting the true meaning of the landscape are usually dotted along the scenic route. In some cases, ornamental images painted on the walls in different sections combine to form a coherent, ongoing story line to add intrigue and interest to the tour, one of the best examples being the pebble pavement in the Imperial Garden of the Forbidden City.

145

Corridor

Fig. 147 A zigzag corridor of the Humble Administrator's Garden, Suzhou. The zigzag is echoed in the pattern of cobblestones that make up the floor.

Fig. 148 A section of a corridor in the Yuyuan Garden, Shanghai.

As a narrow passage that connects the architectural structures in a garden, the corridor forms part of the scenic route. The tourists walk up and down as the corridor rises and falls, creating the effect of a changing scenery with each step. Compared to the other sections of the scenic route, the roofed corridor provides shelter from rain and sun, truly an ideal location to enjoy the sound of the rain and the beauty of the snow. What's more, the corridor serves as an additional scenic route by blending into the various architectural styles of the garden, and by combining its own one-dimensional view with the multifaceted views of halls and pavilions.

147

148

149

Intersection

In traditional Chinese gardens, such architectural
structures as halls, pavilions, and terraces are often
located at intersections where several paths meet and
used as places of relaxation, the most notable being
the small square-shaped pavilion in the Lion Grove
Garden.

*Fig. 149 The Green Shade Hall of
the Lingering Garden in Suzhou.
Trees, creepers on the buildings,
even lichen, and self-sown
plants in the stonework, are all
reflected in the water below.
The stream widens out so that a
visitor could stop on the bridge,
rest, and take in the view.*

Fig. 150 The Huanxiu Mountain Villa, Suzhou, has rocks, a mountain climbing path, stone structures, cliffs, and streams. The richness of the scene goes without saying.

Rock Garden

To some extent, the rock garden is what makes the Chinese garden unique, with some as tall as a towering peak and dominating the garden as a whole, and with others as small as a miniature bonsai and an attraction in its own right.

The rockery in the Huanxiu Mountain Villa in Suzhou, for instance, contains a winding path 70 meters (230 feet) long, all in a small area of a little over 300 square meters (3,230 square feet). The caves, cells, cliffs, and peaks form a delightful "opposite view" with the halls, marble boats, towers, and pavilions in the vicinity.

Waterway

In a garden or park that features water, the waterway forms a substantial part of its scenic route. After all, the view from a rowing boat is dramatically different than that from a bank. Visitors on the water can get a more panoramic view of the garden landscape, particularly at a great distance.

In South China where the parks and gardens are fairly small, those that feature water are far greater in number than in North China. The private garden of the Liu Village near the West Lake, for example, takes full advantage of its location to build a ferry next to the world famous destination, by which visitors can go boating on the West Lake. Most of the imperial gardens in North China, by contrast, are large parks with extensive stretches of water. The Kunming Lake in the Summer Palace, among others, offers visitors a wide range of visual experiences as they move along the waterway from the lake center to the Back Lake, where the view of fields and the countryside, the grandeur of Longevity Hill, and the hustle and bustle of Suzhou Street provide an intriguing sequence of dramatically different views.

Fig. 151 One view of the Qushui Garden in the Qingpu District of Shanghai. The edges of eaves face each other across the river, presenting a feeling of a waterside in the country.

151

HIGHLIGHTS OF CLASSICAL CHINESE GARDENS

Within a sense of basic order, Chinese gardens display highly diversified forms. To enhance garden views, architectural elements and nature are blended in such a way as to present unique visual effects. In both the imperial and private gardens, the buildings display a rich variety of appearance, style, and scale, both horizontally and vertically.

The Imperial Garden in the Forbidden City

First constructed in the 15th year of Emperor Yongle's reign (1403–1424) during the Ming Dynasty, the imposing Forbidden City was where state affairs were administered and grand ceremonies were held. Located in the northernmost part of the central north-south axis of the Forbidden City, the Imperial Garden was built after the traditional architectural pattern of "the palace in the front and the garden at the back." Unlike the other buildings in the Forbidden City, the Imperial Garden offers a relaxing ambience, like a bejeweled court dress, magnificent but not excessive.

The garden measures approximately 130 meters (427 feet) east to west by 90 meters (295 feet) north to south, equally divided into three sections—central, eastern, and western. According to rule, imperial palace gardens should follow the established architectural style of the imperial court and match the surrounding colors. That is why the structures along the east-west axis basically mirror each other: the Floating Green Jade Pavilion (Fubi Pavilion) in the northeast corner with the Pavilion of Pure Felicity (Chengrui Pavilion) in the west, and the Pavilion of Ten Thousand Springs (Wanchun Pavilion) in the middle with the Pavilion of One Thousand Autumns (Qianqiu Pavilion). While the early garden architects emphasized symmetry, they also sought every possible means to avoid

Fig. 152 A water vessel mounted on a dragon in the rockwork of the Imperial Garden of the Forbidden City.

Fig. 153 The Qin'an Hall inside the Imperial Garden, an important ceremonial building where Ming and Qing emperors offered sacrifices.

Fig. 154 Vertical elevations of the magnificent Qianqiu Pavilion and Wanchun Pavilion in the Imperial Garden. The domes are round at the top but square at the bottom, suggestive of the Chinese view of the universe.

Fig. 155 The Yujing Pavilion's Duixiu Hill, the highest point in the rock garden.

Fig. 156 The open Chengrui Pavilion is dedicated to winter use, and its pair is the Fubi (Summer) Pavilion.

Fig. 157 Bird's eye view of the magnificent roofscapes in the Imperial Garden, with the circular Wanchun Pavilion in the center.

monotony. For example, the Studio of Cultivation of Temperament (Yangxing Studio), a two-story pavilion in the corner of the Veranda of Crimson Snow (Jiangxue Veranda), was constructed in a U-shape, entirely different from the T-shaped buildings in the east, which strike the balance between *yin* and *yang* (two opposing elements in nature like negative and positive or feminine and masculine). Another example would be the rock gardens in the southwest corner in front of the Pavilion of Cultivation of Temperament and those at the Hills of High Elegance in the north, which face each other from north to south and east to west across a great distance, orderly but not rigid.

Since the Imperial Garden is fairly small in size, the architectural structures within the garden grounds are densely packed. To highlight the Hall of Imperial Peace (Qin'an Hall, the main building), the surrounding wall is kept lower than usual and the structures along the eastern and western axis are less massive. Most structures are surrounded by walls, with the

solid barrier punctuated only by a small number of exquisite pavilions and terraces leading into the garden, so as to provide a sense of space. In addition, grotesquely shaped rocks, jade seats, gilded unicorns, bronze statues, potted flowers, and bonsai trees are set out to enhance the view. Also noteworthy are the paths elaborately paved with pebbles of different colors, featuring more than 900 patterned images of figures, flowers, plants, sights, dramas, and classical allusions.

Currently there are more than 160 ancient trees in the garden, mostly evergreens like pines and cypresses, creating an air of solemnity. Often found in royal edifices in northern China, pines and cypresses grow tall and narrow (fastigiate) which fits perfectly with the scale of this garden. Their dark green foliage contrasts nicely with the golden rooftops to accentuate the monumentality. Unlike trees in ordinary gardens, the evergreens planted here strictly follow an orderly and symmetrical pattern of planting.

155

156

The Peace and Longevity Palace Garden in the Forbidden City

Built between the 37th and 41st years of Emperor Qianlong's reign (1735–1795), the Peace and Longevity Palace Garden, also known as Qianlong Garden, was prepared for future use by Emperor Qianlong after his abdication in favor of his son.

One of the most expertly designed and constructed gardens within the Forbidden City, the Qianlong Garden is divided into five courtyards all basically symmetrical to each other. Measuring 160 meters (525 feet) north to south by less than 40 meters (131 feet) east to west, it covers only 0.64 hectare. Although densely packed with buildings, the five self-contained, small-sized courtyards each present a specific architectural style that helps create the illusion of a larger place.

Compact but flexible, the architectural framework of the garden boldly alternates curves and angles, creating diverse atmospheres within the complex. The designers used many different elements—vertical and horizontal, symmetrical and non-symmetrical, and different heights and levels, to make this garden full of visual excitement. This variety makes the garden seem larger than actually it is. Its atmosphere is quite distinct from any other part of the area inside the massive walls of the Forbidden City.

The Gate of Spreading Happiness (Yanqi Gate) leads visitors into the first courtyard of the Peace and Longevity Palace Garden. The first sight that meets the eye is an artificial hill built from Taihu rocks. Functioning as a screen wall, the arrangement of the rocks suggests that the door opens onto a view of mountains. Further inside is the south-facing Pavilion of Ancient Flowers (Guhua Pavilion) nestling among green trees in the same courtyard with Xishang Pavilion and the Studio of Restraint (Yi Studio). All of these buildings are grouped close together, but there is no sense of overcrowding. To the west is a walkway

Fig. 158 The Songxiu Pavilion above the rockwork of the Qianlong Garden at the Peace and Longevity Palace (Ningshou Palace) constructed in the years 1771–76 by Emperor Qianlong for his retirement within the Forbidden City.

Fig. 159 Steps up to the Fuwang Pavilion in the Qianlong Garden.

159

161

Fig. 160 A longitudinal cross-section of the Qianlong Garden, where the complexity of the design is evident. The garden covers little more than 5,900 square meters (19,357 square feet), and is no more than 37 meters (121 feet) wide. The artistry of the design creates the sense of a much larger space, with numerous small, jewel-like courtyards. Towering rock gardens provide a sense of vertical space for this compact ground plan.

Fig. 161 Vertical view of the Xishang Pavilion where water meanders along a stone channel in the floor, following the plan for the Orchid Pavilion devised by the ancient sage of calligraphy, Wang Xizhi.

leading to the Stream of the Floating Cup, which is supposedly modeled after the elegantly winding canal depicted in *Prelude for the Pavilion of Cymbidium* by Wang Xizhi, a famous calligrapher of the distant past. The most spacious courtyard in the garden, it offers a sense of solitude, hence the nickname "the Little Garden within the Peace and Longevity Palace Garden."

The Hall of Fulfillment of Original Wishes (Suichu Hall), in the second courtyard, is actually a traditional *siheyuan*, or a walled quadrangle residence. Faced with gray brick, the walls stand on a Rosso Salome marble foundation, lending a rural feel to the setting.

Notable for its exceptionally fine large rocks, the third courtyard is dominated by a sense of strong solid structures, with pavilions, towers, and verandas. The Pavilion of the Three Friends (Sanyou Pavilion), among others, features the contrasting patterns of pine,

bamboo, and plum blossom motifs, all suggestive of picturesque mountains.

In the middle of the fourth courtyard is the Fuwang Pavilion, the most substantial structure in the garden. Enclosed by mountain rocks, the front yard is linked by a covered walkway to the living area at the back, creating a delightful variety of perspectives. One of the major tourist attractions in the Qianlong Garden, Fuwang Pavilion rests on a square-shaped foundation, five rooms wide and five rooms deep, furnished with a stepped, pyramid roof and a covered walkway. The eaves and ridges are decorated with blue glazed tiles that contrast well with yellow-tiled roofs. Seen from the outside, the pavilion looks like a two-story building, but actually it consists of three tiers, whose interior is so lavishly furnished and ingeniously partitioned that visitors usually find themselves lost in a maze of doors and thresholds, hence the name "the

162

Labyrinth Building." On the third floor of the pavilion, a balustraded veranda looks out over the entire Forbidden City.

Quite a number of structures here, including the Yi Studio, the Pavilion of Lush Scenery (Cuishang Pavilion), and the Pavilion of Jade Purity (Yucui Xuan), house Buddhist chapels: Emperor Qianlong held the belief that gardens should serve religious purposes. In other words, religious practice should be performed in a garden setting to meet the aesthetic ideals of the traditional Chinese culture. For an emperor ready to retreat from worldly cares, however, there could be no better themes than leisure and relaxation for such a garden.

The Qianlong Garden is basically a dry garden, a consequence of its precise location within the Forbidden City. With extraordinary skill, the land-scapers were ingenious enough to create the illusion of a larger space by using various architectural forms like walkways and walls, and by building rock gardens in three totally different styles. Topped with brightly colored glazed tiles, most roofs in the garden seem to be strung together, winding their way around the central axis, leaving the impression of a landscape as elegantly intimate as a private garden, and yet as grandiosely splendid as befits an imperial palace.

Fig. 162 Vertical view of the combination of rockwork, the Biluo Pavilion, and the Fuwang Pavilion.

Beihai Park

A glance to the west from the east side of Jingshan Street will give you a clear view of the White Tibetan Pagoda inside Beihai Park, or literally, "North Sea." Centrally located in downtown Beijing, Beihai Park contributes more to the urban landscape than any other imperial garden.

The North Sea river system was developed from the old water course of the original Yongding River. Over the centuries, the river retreated to its present course, further to the south, leaving behind a great expanse of ponds and swamps. Ever since the Liao Dynasty (907–1125), construction of imperial gardens have been going on in this area. Successive emperors have stayed in Beihai to escape the summer heat and for pleasure since the Yuan Dynasty, when the park was converted into the imperial inner garden. The royal families of the Qing Dynasty, however, used the park less, since they found it hard to adapt themselves to the hot summers in Beijing.

Like Zhongnanhai (Central and Southern Seas), Beihai was built as "one pool and three hills," a traditional Chinese principle for building artificial mountains and water works, and also as a true reflection of the dynastic emperors' wish to live an immortal life in the divine seas and celestial mountains. Although most emperors of the past dynasties followed the same principles, they had their gardens built to suit their own wishes, and in terms of a site's potential for making a garden.

To highlight the main features of the garden, the landscapers placed the Jade Flowery (Qionghua) Islet, the central tourist attraction of Beihai, right at the center, where the White Pagoda towers above those monasteries stretching down from the southern hilltop to an archway near the bank. At the southern tip, a bridge connects the islet with the imposing Hall of Receiving Light (Chengguang Hall) in the Circular City (Tuancheng), forming a delightful contrast with the summit and ridge of the southern hill in the distance. Scattered among these peaceful, rolling hills are pavilions and terraces that display an array of inviting colors and styles.

Surrounded by clear water, the Jade Flowery Islet covers an area of nearly 7 hectares. Legend has it that jade flowers grew on the precious trees on the Penglai celestial island. Supposedly, anyone who ate such flowers would be forever young. The island here, as a result, was modeled after the legendary fairyland. Within this imposing palace garden, the central axis of the Jade Flowery Islet is aligned with that of the highest peak, creating a picturesque view, and forming a focus for the landscape that runs along its length. Artificial structures rise on the gentle southern slope while

164

Fig. 165 The White Pagoda is a typical reversed bowl-like tower designed by an eminent monk from Nepal, but the Jingang Hall in front of it gives Chinese character to the ensemble.

Fig. 166 The Five Pavilion Bridge, designed after the bridge at the slender West Lake of Yangzhou, in Jiangsu province, in eastern China. With its stocky columns and low roof, here it is more northern in character and so accords better with the atmosphere of imperial gardens.

Fig. 167 The Haopu Pavilion built in 1757 on the northeast of the Jade Flowery Islet is one of the great attractions of Beihai Park.

166

Fig. 168 The Nine Dragon Wall
in Beihai Park.

Fig. 169 View of the Heart-Ease
Study in Beihai Park, a garden
within a garden.

Fig. 170 The best route for
visiting Beihai Park is crossing
the bridge over the water,
through the memorial gateway,
and up to the White Pagoda.

enticing natural sites dot the steep northern slope. By creating a different ambience in each area, by altering the landforms, and increasing or decreasing the degree of slope on the hillside, the ancient landscapers successfully added a special appeal to the garden.

Erected in the 8th year of Emperor Shunzhi (1643–1661) during the early Qing period, the White Pagoda, a Tibetan Lamaist structure, serves as the landmark of the entire garden. Resting on a huge Buddhist-style brick and stone base, the pagoda rises 35.9 meters (118 feet) high. In the middle of the three circular truncated cones is a shield-shaped niche carved into the facade. The top of the tower is crowned with a bronze umbrella and embellished with bronze bells. Looked at from afar, the pagoda, set amid lush green planting, stands proudly on the summit of the island and overlooks the whole garden. It towers above other buildings around it, presenting an awe-inspiring sight. Symbolically, the White Pagoda represents the inspiring reverence the emperors offered toward religion, and neatly showcases the supremacy of their imperial power.

The Circular City was only a small islet during the Yuan Dynasty. Later, in the Ming period, a city wall was added, and the waterways both east and south of the city were filled in to make land. When the Hall of Receiving Light was reconstructed in the 19th year of the Qing Emperor Kangxi's reign (1661–1722), the original semi-circular dome was converted into an X-shaped structure to highlight the geometric parallelism that echoes the city walls that run down the slopes.

On the eastern and northern banks of the North Sea is a cluster of small gardens. On the east, from south to north in succession, are hills, pools, mounds, and courtyards, culminating in an ingenious combination of views, among which the Haopu Pavilion and the Painted Boat Studio (Huafang Studio) are the most noteworthy. Built in 1758, the Heart-Ease Study (Jingxin Zhai) on the south bank was one of the favorite gardens of Emperor Qianlong, and also the place specially reserved for his crown prince to study. Exquisitely fashioned after the unique style of the scholar's garden south of the Yangtze River, the Heart-Ease Study is considered one of the best preserved examples of its kind, a "Garden of Gardens." Although the building is a broad but short rectangle, the garden makers used rock gardens, covered walkways, and secluded paths to create the feeling of more space, as well as an illusion of a wide variety of distinct landscapes. The mirrorlike "water courtyard" links the square antechamber with the imposing chief room, making a wonderful unison with the lotus pond by the main hall and the Taiye Pool outside the garden. The main courtyard is lively and spacious, in which well chosen rocks and waterscapes create the style of a typical scholar's garden.

Featuring the architectural combinations of "real mountains plus real lakes" and "fluidity plus utility," the imperial North Sea Park successfully realizes the elusive concept of the celestial garden by incorporating the types of temples, monasteries, and scholar's gardens common south of the Yangtze into its own grand concept, offering thereby an epitome of a classical Chinese garden.

169

168

The Summer Palace

Situated in the northwest outskirts of Beijing, the Summer Palace was formerly named the Garden of Clear Ripples (Qingyi Garden). Its construction took 15 years and cost more than 4 million taels of silver. When completed, the Garden of Clear Ripples linked the four neighboring gardens together into an expansive garden belt that stretched over 20 kilometers (12 miles).

Clear Ripples is considered one of the finest gardens to make the best use of natural landscapes. In his *Postscript to the Old Summer Palace*, Emperor Qianlong thought so highly of his summer residence that he decreed no more gardens should be built thereafter. But later he changed his mind—with two high-sounding excuses: one was the imperative need to reconstruct the river system in the northwestern suburbs; the other was the need to prepare a special birthday gift for his mother. As a result, the original West Lake was substantially enlarged, and the vast quantity of earth removed in the process of enlargement was piled up upon nearby hills. A causeway was also built to divide the lake into three sections, each with an island in the middle to follow the architectural principle of "one pool and three hills." Notably, however, the new palace essentially retained the original layout of the Garden of Clear Ripples.

Such extensive construction, not surprisingly, had much to do with the reigning emperor himself. Qianlong would never tour South China without visiting or staying in famous gardens. Moreover, he would order the court artists to paint these gardens for his own reference, and the Garden of Clear Ripples was, naturally enough, the culmination of his consistent and deep interest. Covering an area of 279 hectares, Qianlong's garden was imposingly majestic, definitely a cut above those private gardens that condensed the world into a small space. Among the various architectural forms were temples, precincts, shopping streets, bridges, wharfs, pavilions, terraces, storied

buildings, pagodas, and towers that suggested famous mountains. In addition, the planning of the Garden of Clear Ripples focused on achieving an overall environment of "three mountains and five gardens," rather than just the palace complex itself. To maintain the landscape integrity, the west bank of the lake was free from palace walls, thus enabling people in the garden to enjoy views of the countryside and the beautiful Garden of Tranquility and Brightness (Jingming Garden). A masterful plan indeed!

Basically, the entire garden can be divided into three sections: the court area, the frontal aspect of the hill facing the lake, and the rear aspect of the hill looking out on the lake. Located to the east of Longevity Hill, the court area can be further divided into the outer and inner court. The outer court contains the Gateway and Palace of Benevolence and Longevity as well as the subsidiary buildings. The inner court, west of the outer court, was the imperial residence, including

Fig. 171 Bird's eye view of the Front Hill of the Summer Palace.

Fig. 172 The Seventeen-Arch Bridge connecting the South Lake Island and the east bank.

Fig. 173 *The Long Corridor in the Summer Palace.*

the Hall of Jade Ripples (Yulan Hall, the emperor's bed chamber), Chamber of Fragrant Grasses (Yiyun Chamber, the empress's bed chamber), and Hall of Happiness and Longevity (Leshou Hall, bed chamber of the emperor's mother). Of these residences, the Hall of Happiness and Longevity is the largest, and the Chamber of Fragrant Grasses is the smallest, suggestive of the political situation where Empress Dowager Cixi exercised her overwhelming power over the government and the empire in those days. To the west of the Hall of Happiness and Longevity is a vast imperial park, with the ridge of Longevity Hill as the demarcation line between two scenic areas.

The frontal aspect looks out on the expansive Kunming Lake, a replica of the West Lake in Hangzhou, with the long West Causeway extending into the water. Three larger islands (Nanhu Island, Zaojian Hall, and Zhijing Pavilion) and three smaller ones are scattered in the lake. The buildings produce an integrated landscape view. Geometrically, the Spring Heralding Pavilion and the Zaojian Hall establish a visual connection with the towering peaks of the Jade Spring Mountain (Yuquan Mountain) and the Red Mountain Pass (Hongshan Gran) in the far distance. To avoid blocking the view, the West Causeway, the northwest and due west sections of Kunming Lake are free from all tall buildings. There are, in fact, no other buildings west of the front hill except for bridges. Accordingly, a striking contrast is formed between high and low building density, as

well as between bright colors and delicate hues of the buildings and garden areas.

To reach Longevity Hill from the lake shore, visitors have to walk past white marble balustrades, cypress groves, and long wooded paths, until they reach the Long Corridor. Altogether, the Long Corridor comprises 273 bays, with a total length of 728 meters (2,388 feet). The beams and rafts are painted with more than 14,000 colorful images of various themes. Symbolizing the four seasons of a year, four pavilions along the corridor punctuate the longest covered walkway in the world as it zigzags its way to the Hall of Dispelling Clouds.

Centrally located on Longevity Hill is a large architectural complex used for both administrative and religious purposes—the Gate of Dispelling Clouds (Paiyun Gate), Hall of Dispelling Clouds (Paiyun Hall), and Pavilion of the Fragrance of the Buddha (Foxiang Pavilion). These structures, tier raised upon tier, massive yet refined, follow the contours of the hillside, all looking out over the garden. Taken together, the complex measures 160 meters (525 feet) east to west by 210 meters (690 feet) north to south, and stands as the landmark of the front hill area.

The rear hill and rear lake section, in fact, refers to a waterway between the foot of the hill and the palace wall, taking up 12 percent of the garden grounds. The rear lake winds its way through the artificial rock gardens on the north bank and the real hills on the south, presenting a set of delightful views. In the middle of

174

the waterway is a little group of shops built in the style of a typical street south of the Yangtze River. Here the children, grandchildren, and women members of the imperial family confined within the palace walls were able to experience the pleasures of shopping—just like ordinary people.

On the middle section of the back hill area rises Mount Meru, an architectural complex of Buddhist temples, which forms a north-south axis together with the Three-Arched Stone Bridge spanning the middle of the back lake and the North Palace Gate. Following the contours of the hillside, the temples here combine both Han and Tibetan architectural styles. The Temple of Fragrant Stones, the main building of the complex, stands out for both its monumental scale and splendid decoration, forming a sharp contrast with the typical traditional inland Buddhist temples that emphasize horizontal extension rather than vertical elevation.

Nestling at the foot of Longevity Hill, the Garden of Harmonious Interests is a small, exquisite, and self-contained complex built by Emperor Qianlong after the Jichang Garden at the base of the Huishan Mountain in Wuxi, in East China's Jiangsu Province. Peaceful and rustic, on the eastern side of the hill, this charming garden is centered on a pool, with buildings distributed symmetrically on four sides. All of the scenic spots are linked by a covered walkway, with larger spaces at the points where the walkway turns. One of the places most frequently used by Emperor Qianlong, it offers a striking contrast with those huge and majestic edifices on Longevity Hill.

On the front hill, cypress trees far outnumber pines, whose dark green shapes contrast well with the golden rooftops of the surrounding palaces, halls, and pavilions, thus enhancing the stupendous view of the royal palace on the front hill. To highlight the effect of seasonal foliage, more pines were planted on the rear hill than cypresses, and these were interspersed with deciduous trees, bushes, and shrubs, to form large tracts of peaceful woodland.

Fig. 174 Originally called Merchants' Street, this imitated the shops in the busy city of Suzhou, and was built on the orders of Emperor Qianlong. It was destroyed by the British and French armies in 1860 and restored in 1990.

Fig. 175 The Paiyun Hall among the trees and the Foxiang Pavilion on the hillside are the main sites of the Front Hill of the Summer Palace. At the top of the hill, the Hall of the Sea of Wisdom is a Buddhist temple with a panoramic view over the whole garden.

Fig. 176 The Garden of Harmonious Interests (Xieq Garden) was first made by Emperor Qianlong beside the Kunming Lake of the Summer Palace. It was inspired by his visit in 1751 to the famous Jichang Garden in Wuxi. It was destroyed in 1860, but was fully restored in 1893 to its original splendor. The Garden of Harmonious Interests exemplifies all of the design techniques of the great gardens of the south, with perhaps a greater sense of drama.

Fig. 177 The open hall of the Huacheng Pavilion and the buildings around it.

176

177

Fig. 178 *The buildings at the side of the Foxiang Pavilion.*

Fig. 179 *The Marble Boat.*

Fig. 180 *View across the water in the Garden of Harmonious Interests. The Zhiyu Bridge and the buildings along the waterline unite to create an image of harmony.*

The Chengde Summer Resort

In the 20th year of Emperor Kangxi's reign (1661–1722), the Qing government built the vast Mulan Hunting Ground beyond the Great Wall. After that, during his yearly tour of North China, Emperor Kangxi would stay there for the great annual hunting expedition, the Mulan Autumn Chase. In 1703, Kangxi went so far as to order the construction of the huge Imperial Summer Villa at Jehol (Chengde). Later on, Emperor Qianlong had it dramatically enlarged, with the addition of the Outlying Eight Temples outside the park.

The Summer Resort is an exceptional complex that makes best use of the existing landscape features but the design also takes advantage of very favorable natural conditions for creating a superlative garden. Having learned from the traditional garden landscapes made in South China, Emperor Kangxi began his project with excavating riverbeds, draining wetlands, diverting water courses, and forming man-made islands in the lakes, so that the entire garden was linked together by its waterways. In addition, he had the mountain streams channeled to create waterfalls, so that the gurgling and gushing of running water made the secluded mountains come alive with the sounds of nature.

Extending over 564 hectares, the Summer Resort contains two principal sections: the court area and the garden area. The garden can be further divided into three zones: lake, plain, and mountain.

Formerly the administrative and residential quarters for the Qing emperors during their stays in Jehol, the court area consists of the Main Palace, the Pine-Crane Temple, the Sighing Pines Valley, and the East Palace. Covering one hectare, the Main Palace contains nine courtyards. The Hall of Simplicity and Sincerity, the principle structure of the palace, was where the emperors dealt with state affairs and held grand ceremonies. It is also known as the Nanmu Hall, since the edifice is built entirely of *nanmu*, a precious,

rot-resistant hardwood used for furniture, boat building, and carving. The Sighing Pines Valley refers to a self-contained garden complex north of the Pine-Crane Temple. The main hall, a five-bay-wide structure surrounded by a covered corridor, was where Emperor Kangxi read reports, received his ministers, and took his ease reading the classics of Chinese literature. Built on a hilltop and facing a lake on the north side, the whole complex was superbly designed to offer a unique panoramic view.

As the major scenic attraction of the Summer Resort, the lake area is divided by causeways and islands into several parts, while the overall extent is only slightly less than Kunming Lake in the Summer

Fig. 181 The eight arches of the Shuixin Pavilion stand on a causeway across a lake at the Imperial Mountain Summer Resort of Chengde. This is the largest of all the imperial gardens, covering more than twice the area of the Summer Palace in Beijing.

Fig. 182 The inscription above the main gate of the Imperial Mountain Summer Resort.

182

Palace of Beijing. The whole area is interlinked with bridges, and the banks are lined with leafy trees, offering an enticing setting. Architecturally, the overall layout is a complex of structures ingeniously built on the banks, islets, and mountains, where hills, islands, and waters meet and interconnect with each other to present a picturesque impression of a waterside village. Most of the architecture here is modeled, in one way or another, after those famous sites in South China. Most notably, the Pavilion of Mist and Rain was built in the 46th year of Emperor Qianlong's reign (1735–1795) after the Pavilion of Mist and Rain at Jiaxing of Zhejiang Province. Centrally located on the Green Lotus Islet (Qinglian Islet), the pavilion is a range of massive, two-story terraces, complemented by gateways, verandas, and covered walkways, and overall creating an amazing array of colors and contours against the silvery ripples of the lake. The complex fits perfectly within the overall landscape of the north lake, an example of "a garden within a garden" that makes the best use of both the local topographical features and the wider landscape. Not surprisingly,

the largest island of the lake area is an S-shaped hill named Ruyi, with, right at the center, the Mountainous Residence of Prolonged Warmth (Yanxun Shanguan). It was here, before the Main Palace was dedicated, that Emperor Kangxi lived and ruled China.

North of the lake, the flat open plain includes both grassland and woodland. Centuries before, there used to be the Garden of Ten Thousand Trees (Wanshu Garden), where all the structures were built in the style of Mongolian yurts, like a miniature of the Mulan Hunting Ground that blends well with the distant grasslands north of the Great Wall.

The mountain area consists of four heavily forested north-south gullies to the northeast of the Summer Resort, where towering pines blanket the rolling hills. Between the northwest peak and the southeast wetland and plain, there is a rise of 180 meters (590 feet) sheltering the east of the resort from hot summers and cold winters. Under Emperor Qianlong, many gardens and temples were constructed on the mountain slopes, including most of the Outlying Eight Temples. These were built on the sunny side, where

Han- and Tibetan-style palaces and halls tower above the surrounding landscape. To highlight the fact that the Outlying Eight Temples and the Summer Resort are a unified whole, each temple was made to point its central axis toward the Summer Resort, symbolizing the friendly relations between the ethnic groups in the frontier region and the central government of the Qing Empire.

Historically, the Summer Resort is the result of the combined efforts of three successive emperors, namely Kangxi, Yongzheng, and Qianlong, although each of them had his own aspirations and priorities for this vast estate. While Emperor Kangxi, founder of the Summer Resort, preferred simple architecture to magnificent edifices, Qianlong had elaborate ideas of successful landscaping and chose to have his garden lavishly decorated. What we see in the largest of all the imperial gardens is a melange of architectural styles, taken from both South and North China. The combined efforts of the three emperors created a mountain paradise of waterscapes, gardens, and cool seductive woods.

183

Fig. 184 A replica of Golden Mount Temple in Zhejiang, erected at Chengde.

Fig. 185 A stone bank from which to watch fish in the Imperial Mountain Summer Resort, a simple structure built in the reign of Emperor Kangxi.

Fig. 186 A copy of the Lion Grove Garden at Suzhou, in the Imperial Mountain Summer Resort built in the reign of Emperor Qianlong.

Fig. 187 The grand temple of the Potaraka Doctrine built at Chengde between 1767 and 1771. It was closely modeled on the Potala Palace in Lhasa, Tibet, one of the most holy sites of Tibetan Buddhism.

184

185

The Humble Administrator's Garden

Located at Suzhou, in East China's Jiangsu province, the Humble Administrator's Garden is known as one of the best four gardens in Suzhou. First built by a Ming Dynasty official, Wang Xianchen, who retired to his home village after falling out of favor with the government, this ensemble covers more than 4 hectares. Interestingly, it was named after an essay, *On Idle Living*, by Pan Yue of the Jin Dynasty (265–420), who suggested that a "politically naive" official might just as well idle his time away by growing vegetables. This wonderful garden was Wang Xianchen's comment, part subtle self-mockery, but also self-justification, for the garden he created, which was indeed the better outcome of a life's work than an official career.

The Humble Administrator's Garden is a backyard garden, connected to the house in front by several passageways. The whole area is set around an exquisite waterscape that complements and blends with the overall landscape design. If you enter through the waist-high south gate and walk around a yellow rock garden, you will be greeted by the main building—the Hall of Drifting Fragrance (Yuanxiang Hall). This is only a short distance from a large lotus pond, where a faint scent of lotus flowers drifts in the air, offering an exceptionally peaceful setting.

A glance to the north from the hall reveals an artificial island built from earth excavated from the pond. A stream cuts through the island, dividing it into two portions. Over the stream is a small stone-slab bridge, adding a mysterious feel to the peaceful landscape. Trees and plants grow so well here that they form a varied skyline. The hilltop of the island is crowned by the Prunus Mume Pavilion, which is intended to give the impression of a small inn of a mountain village. Facing each other across the pond, the pavilion and the Hall of Drifting Fragrance form a central axis, along which most of the garden's attractions are located. On the west shore, the Tower of Mountain View seems

to be floating on the pond. When visitors enjoy the view from the Hall of Drifting Fragrance, the pavilion becomes a backdrop to the garden. Lying to the south is the Fragrant Continent, a boat hall with a pavilion in the front and a tower at the back, connected by a line of low-rise buildings.

Quite a number of winding bridges span the pond, which is fed by a stream from the south that flows to a half-pavilion. Over the stream is an arc-shaped

Fig. 188 External view of the Jianshan Tower in the Humble Administrator's Garden, Suzhou, in early spring.

Fig. 189 The inscription over the main gate of the Humble Administrator's Garden says the garden symbolized the "administration engaged in by a humble man."

189

Fig. 190 Elevation of the
Xiangzhou building in the
Humble Administrator's
Garden , built on the Fragrant
Isle to resemble a boat floating
on the water.

Fig. 191 The Jianshan Tower
under snow in winter.

Fig. 192 Inside Thirty-six
Mandarin Ducks Hall.

covered bridge named Small Flying Rainbow. The framed scenery of the bridge, the sunlit roofscape overhead, and reflections under the bridge form a delightful contrast. Also noteworthy is the Small Pavilion of Surging Waves on the pond, a variant of the covered bridge, which offers a very appealing view of a waterside village. Although the stream does not run far, the two covered bridges in between naturally create an illusion of increased length.

East of the Hall of Drifting Fragrance are several exquisitely designed "gardens within gardens," primarily used as transitional landscape. Most notably, the Malus Spring Castle justifies its name by planting *Malus micromalus* and using crabapple-shaped decor and floor patterns. A small tree stands in each of the two small yards flanking the castle. Looked at from different angles, the view is dramatically different, although the tree is always the same.

The western part of the Humble Administrator's Garden is also known as the Supplementary Garden. Walking through the tunnel portal, visitors are greeted by the elegant, fan-shaped With Whom Shall I Sit? Pavilion. It was named after a poem by Su Dongpo: "With whom shall I sit? Bright moon, cool wind, and myself." The feeling of aloofness and melancholy is magnified by the illusion of increased distance across the pond. Arguably, the most impressive sight here is the waterside walkway that overhangs the water, and zigzags its way, adding interest to the pond.

Other major structures of the garden include the Listen to the Rain Pavilion in the southeast and Stay and Listen Pavilion in the west. Although both were named after the same line by the Tang poet Li Shangyin ("Withered lotus is left alone to listen to the rain"), the former stresses *listening* to the sound of rain, while the latter pays more attention to *left alone*, suggesting that viewers should enjoy flowers before they fade and die.

Architecturally, the Humble Administrator's Garden can be considered a wonderful example of a large garden that features movement, with a wealth of forking and dividing paths through it, splendid viewpoints, and constant variations on the sense of space. The greatest success comes from the harmonious contrast of landscapes: the main scenic area around the waterscape creates the impression of a much larger space, which is further enhanced by the auxiliary scenic areas densely packed with buildings. Moreover, "borrowed view" plays a significant role here, as evidenced by the fact that the Temple Pagoda in the north of Suzhou is clearly visible from the garden.

190

Fig. 193 The view from the lattice window over the east garden.

Fig. 194 The Qixiu Pavilion beside the loquat garden.

The Great Gardens of China

Fig. 195 The Yuanxiang Hall is
the main building in the Humble
Administrator's Garden. The
scent of the lotus covering the
water explains its name.

Fig. 196 The graceful curve of the
Small Flying Rainbow Bridge.

The Master-of-Nets Garden

First built at the end of the 12th century during the Southern Song Dynasty, the Master-of-Nets Garden in Suzhou is a 0.4-hectare complex of three courtyards, located immediately west of the main hall, with its principal courtyard set around a lake. Metaphorically, the master-of-nets is a fisherman, suggestive of a form of detachment from worldly cares.

On entering the garden gate, visitors are captivated by the Study of the Recluse's cassia woods, whose name alludes to a line from Liu An's poem, "Summons for a Recluse": "The cassia trees grow thick in the mountain's recesses." Cloudy Hill, a rock garden north of the study, is built of yellow stones. Crowned with yellow cassia flowers, the hill screens the lake from

view. (According to traditional Chinese architectural principles, a massive and sometimes noisy building used for social gatherings should be placed some distance away from the waterscape.)

West of the study is a belvedere called Waterside Belvedere for Washing One's Hat Strings. This name also alludes to a line from an ancient poem, suggestive of the adaptability of a retired official to the varied circumstances: "When the waters are clear, / I can wash my hat-strings in them; / When the waters are muddy, / I can wash my feet in them." A covered walkway leads to The Moon Rises and the Wind Stirs, a hexagonal pavilion on the lake and one of the most evocative sights of the garden. Architecturally, the

Fig. 197 Inside the Dianchun Room in the small Master-of-Nets Garden (Wangshi Garden), Suzhou. "Borrowed views" through windows or grilles are a key element in the design.

Fig. 198 The buildings at the northeast corner of the water in the Master-of-Nets Garden. The mixture of different forms cleverly relieves the sense of compression where twenty-two buildings and a pool crowd into a small space.

198

Figs. 199–200 Fine calligraphy
is a notable feature of the
garden.

Fig. 201 The majestic gate to the
inner court in the Master-of-
Nets Garden.

Fig. 202 View of the west bank
of the pool in the Master-of-
Nets Garden, centered on the
enticing Where the Wind Meets
the Moon Pavilion, reflected in
the still water.

scenic vistas around the lake are all examples of open-ended—yet relatively self-contained—spaces built on low foundations around waterscapes.

Watching Pines and Reading Paintings and Gathered Emptiness, the two studios north of the lake, serve as the main residential area. One of the most important attractions in the garden, Gathered Emptiness is a two-story tower that overlooks the whole complex. Bamboo Branch Beyond, a covered walkway in front of the studio, was constructed to minimize the massiveness of the tower. Of special note is the ingeniously designed framework of the tower—all connections are positioned at the same height and glued mortise and tenon joints for extra durability.

The Late Spring Studio, a small courtyard in the northeast corner of the garden, derived its name from another well-known poem: "The peonies alone are left to bloom in the late spring wind." That explains why peonies are grown inside the courtyard, interspersed with bamboos and plum and banana trees. The windows of the studio are exceptionally beautiful, like antique picture frames when viewed from the outside.

An extensive rock work embraces three of the walls, facing the Fountain of Overflowing Green. Nearby this tiny but deep pool stands the Cold Spring Pavilion, a half-pavilion typical of Chinese gardens. When the Metropolitan Museum of Art in New York City built its Ming Hall, it modeled the design after the Late Spring Studio, and so the Master-of-Nets Garden has become famous in the Western world.

Recognized as one of the finest of classical gardens in South China, the Master-of-Nets Garden features an ingenious garden arrangement—compact but not crowded. Roughly square shaped as it is, the small pond offers a seemingly endless view of the garden with the winding walkways along its coves in the southeast and northwest corners. Since no weeds or lotus flowers are planted in the pond, its water is sparkling clear—a perfect reflecting pool—and appears wider than it is in reality. Equally important, the pond is about 20 meters (66 feet) wide, just the normal human viewing distance, hence offering a panoramic view of the opposite bank. Peaceful yet full of movement, the garden never fails to mesmerize visitors.

The Lingering Garden

The Lingering Garden in Suzhou was constructed on the site of the East Garden of the Ming Dynasty, built by Xu Taishi, a former minister. During the reign of Emperor Jiaqing (1796–1820) of Qing, the East Garden was reconstructed and renamed the Cold Green Village. Later, it was renamed again as the Lingering Garden, as in Chinese this sounds the same as the surname of its owner, Liu. Meanwhile, a name plaque was added to its entrance, explaining the name with the poetic inscription, "Lingering Forever between Heaven and Earth".

The garden we see today is what remains from the Qing Dynasty. Covering 2 hectares, the whole area can be roughly divided into four parts: what is left of the Cold Green Village in the middle, or the principal part around the lake; the Grand Artificial Hill in the west; the complex of buildings in the east; and an untouched mountain village in the north.

In the heart of the garden, a small island called Little Penglai was created in the pond, linked via a winding footbridge to a peninsula east of the island. North of the pond a hill of rock and earth was piled up with lakebed rocks and yellow stones. On the hill stands a small hexagonal pavilion named Keting Pavilion, which offers a panoramic view of the most strikingly picturesque landscape south of the hill—the Pellucid Tower and the Villa of Overflowing Green.

Fig. 203 The Pellucid Tower (Mingse Tower) of the Lingering Garden in autumn.

Fig. 204 The view of the Keting Pavilion from the Mingse Tower in winter.

Fig. 205 A village in the northern part of Lingering Garden.

204

The western part sets a fine example of attractive earthen hills studded with yellow stones. On the summit of the Grand Artificial Hill, the Shuxiao Pavilion towers above a winding brook lined with peach trees down in the valley. To enhance the height of the hill, walls of the few buildings here are kept very low.

Also known by the name of Nanmu Hall, the Celestial Hall of Five Peaks is the most impressive building of the architectural complex in the east of the garden. The largest of all the halls in Suzhou, it is remarkably spacious and lavishly furnished. The courtyard in the front of the ensemble is named Five Ancient Peaks. When all of its windows are open, the two skylights flanking the hall create an illusion of walking through real mountains and forests. Though buildings are close together here, the Yifeng Studio in the east sits in a peaceful setting. A line of small courtyards south of the studio are interlinked with each other. The Return-to-Read Study, another small courtyard north of the studio, is as delightful as it is secluded. Miraculously it suggests infinity, while at the same time being a labyrinth of small spaces.

In the northeast corner of the garden stands a splendidly decorated double-house named the Old Hermit Scholars' Hall. Nearby, close to a small pond called the Huanyun Pool, stands a Taihu rock called the Cloud-Capped Peak. Over 5 meters (17 feet) tall,

its reflection in the crystal-clear water below and a group of buildings designed to set off its sculptural grandeur add immense charm to the garden. It is the largest limestone in any of the classical gardens in Suzhou, and arguably, the grandest. Perhaps its sheer scale meant that it escaped the attentions of Emperor Huizong of Northern Song (1100–1125), who had a great passion for the finest Taihu rocks and had them carried off to his capital.

The northern part of the garden is named Another Village, now used to exhibit hundreds of specimen plants and potted landscapes. It is otherwise empty, with only a few buildings, to allow the spectator's imagination to roam, like the blank space purposefully left in a traditional Chinese painting.

The covered walkway linking all the scenic spots within the garden is 700 meters (2,300 feet) long, winding with the topography and offering an endlessly changing vista.

Although the four scenic areas of the Lingering Garden display remarkably different features—massive structures alternate with small buildings in complicated landscapes—they share a similar architectural style. Like the Humble Administrator's Garden, the Lingering Garden features well-arranged, man-made landscapes that complement each other and offer constant variety, color, and interest.

Fig. 206 The tall and elegant Cloud-Capped Peak rock in the Lingering Garden. In front of the rock, the Huanyun Pool picks up the reflection.

Fig. 207 The vista to the north of the Ke Ting Pavilion.

207

Fig. 208 The interior of the Old Hermit Scholars' Hall in the Lingering Garden, the largest twin-hall in the gardens of Suzhou.

Fig. 209 The southward view from the Wufengxian Hall. Its name derives from the massed rocks outside the window.

Fig. 210 Inside the yard to the west of the small building in the "stone forest" of the Lingering Garden. The rustling leaves of the plantains add to the purely visual impact.

The Surging Waves Pavilion

The Chinese word "garden" has many other common names, one of the most notable being "pavilion," evidence of the important role that pavilions play in a garden. The Surging Waves Pavilion in the south of Suzhou, as its name suggests, is a garden named after the historic pavilion within its grounds. Covering 1.08 hectares, the Surging Waves Pavilion is recognized as the oldest of the existing classical gardens in Suzhou, dating as far back as the Five Dynasties period (907–960). The garden was originally the private property of a prince, but later, during the Northern Song Dynasty, Su Shunqin, a poet-scholar who had fallen out of favor with the government, built his mansion here and named it Canglang, or Surging Waves.

Although it has been rebuilt many times since then, most of the present landscapes are still reminiscent of the original Song Dynasty architectural style.

The Surging Waves Pavilion features a unique layout integrating woods and water. A stream winds through the garden and out the northern gate. A number of self-contained pavilions and terraces are set out along the stream, creating a feeling of wide-open space, and blending perfectly with the cityscape in the distance.

A long covered walkway, east of the main gate, winds its way along the stream from the Waterside Chamber to the Fish-Viewing Pond. Separated by a partition wall, the walkway itself contains two parallel paths punctuated with latticed windows. Taken

Fig. 211 The view of "the emerald green" from the Surging Waves Pavilion. Slim bamboos are planted in the north and south yards, visible both against the white wall and through the grille.

Fig. 212 The waterscape outside the Surging Waves Pavilion extends below the bridge across the whole facade.

212

Fig. 213 The full architectural elevation of the Surging Waves Pavilion above the water: trees, buildings, and open water unite perfectly.

Fig. 214 The Surging Waves Pavilion gets its name from the inscriptions on the pillars.

together, there are 108 different types of latticed windows in the garden, each with its own unique style and pattern.

Created with more earth than stone, and heavily forested with towering trees and thick bushes, the rock formations in the garden offer an ambience of woody hills. Viewed from across the stream, the famous Surging Waves Pavilion, a square-shaped antique, stands proudly on the hilltop. The couplets carved on its stone pillars read: "The refreshing breeze and the bright moon are priceless; The nearby water and the distant mountains strike a sentimental note." Since the Fish-Viewing Pavilion is located closer to the water, with the distant Surging Waves Pavilion in the backdrop, visitors usually mistake it for the main pavilion. Architecturally, however, the Surging Waves Pavilion high on the hilltop overlooks the water across the covered walkway from behind the thick woods, ideally positioned to create an enhanced feeling of peace and serenity.

Also noteworthy is a small but deep pool in the west of the garden, elegantly perched on the hillside to highlight the mountain view.

Bamboos have long been the traditional plant that makes the garden unique ever since it was built by Su Shunqing. Altogether, more than twenty bamboo species are currently grown here. The Jade and Exquisite Study, a spacious complex in the north, comprises exquisitely designed side-chambers of various sizes. Filled with green bamboos and banana and pine trees that dance with shadow and light, both the front- and backyards are alive with movement and color. A glance to the north through the latticed windows from the main hall gives visitors a mesmerizing view of the sunlit bamboo leaves—a sea of fresh green ripples like water and a symphony of soft rustling foliage.

One of the few gardens with a walkway linking all of its spaces, the Surging Waves Pavilion, together with the Lion Grove Garden, the Humble Administrator's Garden, and the Lingering Garden, are the finest examples of the classical Suzhou gardens of the Song, Yuan, Ming, and Qing Dynasty styles.

Fig. 215 Water plays a vital role in the Surging Waves Pavilion complex. A corner in the Surging Waves Pavilion, with the pool to the east and the corridor running around and above the rockwork.

Fig. 216 The fish-watching place to the west of the Mianshui Chamber and open water with scholar trees (Sophora japonica) nearby.

Fig. 217 In the back of the Surging Waves Pavilion.

215

216

The Lion Grove Garden

Dating back some 650 years, the Lion Grove Garden was originally a temple built by Tianru, a prominent monk of the Yuan Dynasty, so named because the grotesque rock formations were said to resemble crouching lions. Ni Zan, a celebrated Yuan Dynasty painter who participated in building the garden, captured its beauty in his masterful painting *Scroll of Lion Grove*, and brought instant fame to the garden.

Covering 1.1 hectares, the Lion Grove is a walled-in garden of irregular shape, with hilly terrain in the southeast and numerous waterscapes in the northwest. Surrounded by long corridors lined with latticed windows, the famous rock garden is perhaps the prime attraction; but also noteworthy are the more

than seventy historic stone tablets and steles with calligraphy inscribed by famous artists.

Compactly set out around the central pool, the architectural structures in the garden are grouped into three parts: the Ancestral Temple, the Residence, and the Courtyard. The Ancestral Temple at the entrance of the garden was once owned by the Pei family, the second largest property owner in Shanghai in the 1920s. Spacious and splendid, Yanyu Hall functions as the main building of the whole residential area, a typical Chinese twin structure that houses a painted screen with *Scroll of Lion Grove* inscribed on one side, and *Record of Restoring the Lion Grove* on the other. In the courtyard north of the hall are planted two

Fig. 218 *The majestic rocks in the Lion Grove Garden, with the marble boat and the Tower of Hidden Fragrance and Sparse Shadow in the background.*

Fig. 219 *Interior of one of the twin-halls—the Yanyu Hall.*

Fig. 220 *Inside the corridor on the western side of the Lion Grove Garden, with hexagonal apertures on the left and grilles on the right.*

Fig. 221 *The Woyun Room surrounded by a rock garden is a striking focus of the garden.*

primrose trees (*Lagunaria patersonii*), an exotic addition to the veritable garden of springtime colors. Most of the attractions here center on the twin structure, with passageways leading to Standing-in-Snow Hall, Lying-in-Clouds Chamber, and a small square-shaped hall named Garden of Tour Delights nearby.

Walking through the square hall, visitors will admire the nine imposing peaks that are said to resemble nine lions in different poses and with different facial expressions. The latticed windows in the courtyard north of the peaks are decorated with fine images of the Chinese lute and chess playing, calligraphy paintings, and flowers. Located on the highest point in the west of the garden, the Flying Waterfall Pavilion is a three-tiered structure built of lakebed rocks, with a water tank installed on top. As soon as the mechanism is switched on, a man-made waterfall comes alive, plunging into the canyon below.

Situated in the west of the garden, the courtyard area consists primarily of the Lotus Hall and Pavilion of Truc Delights, both built close to water and embellished with exquisite wood carvings. An ingeniously designed walkway links the top floor of the Tower

of Hidden Fragrance and Sparse Shadows with the Fan Pavilion, Wen Tianxiang Stele Pavilion, and the Imperial Stele Pavilion—a line of low-rise structures against the massive southern wall. Most of the buildings here are located in the north, all with varying heights and different styles.

Covering an area of 0.15 hectare, the labyrinthine rock garden is considered the most stunning sight of the Lion Grove. Full of movement and mixed textures, designed with a combination of twists and turns, the three-tiered rock garden is piled up with limestone from Taihu Lake in Wuxi City. Visitors easily get lost in its tempting maze of nine winding paths and twenty-one caverns—the end seems close at hand, but in reality it is still far away. While a gully in the west divides the artificial hill into two sections, a bamboo terrace spans the gully like a natural karst cave and joins the two halves into a whole. During his lifetime, Qing Emperor Qianlong toured the Lion Grove Garden six times, and had two similar gardens built in the Forbidden City and the Summer Resort, both modeled after the Lion Grove Garden.

223

Fig. 222 The Waterfall Watching Pavilion on the hill to the west of the garden, where the water within the garden originates.

Fig. 223 The colored glass panes of the little square hall reflect a Western influence. The hall is a transitional space between where the Yanyu Hall and the garden originates.

Fig. 224 The large rockwork seen from the Yifeng Zhibai Chamber, with its jagged rocks and wildly grotesque shapes. The rails and the bridge by the pond in front of the rockwork take Western forms, reflecting the interest of the former 20th-century garden owner.

The Geyuan Garden

The classical gardens in Yangzhou, a city with a long history, combine an ideal mixture of strength and elegance, the two defining properties that characterize traditional gardens in North China and South China. Although Yangzhou gardens are renowned for their fantastic rock formations with seasonal views, the Geyuan Garden is arguably the most telling example of all. Historically, Geyuan Garden used to be the private residence of Huang Yingtai, a salt businessman in the early 19th century. At that time, most wealthy salt businessmen of Yangzhou were educated people who loved working with scholars and collecting calligraphy and painting. As a result, they made great contributions to the development of local art as much as the Medici family of Florence fostered and inspired the birth of the Italian Renaissance.

Geyuan Garden gets its interesting name from the fact that the garden is filled with bamboos—the Chinese character *zhu* (bamboo) is made up of two *ge* Chinese characters. Located behind the house, the Geyuan Garden covers an area of about 0.6 hectare. All the scenic elements are arranged according to seasonal themes. Since spring marks the beginning of a year, signs of spring appear by the main entrance, where two flower beds are carefully laid out, with one displaying white rocks, the other black ones, all towering high into the air above the flowers. West of the entrance and next to the flower beds, springtime colors are further enhanced by dense bamboo groves. Bamboos of different species are planted around these seasonal rock gardens: hairy bamboo for spring, water bamboo for summer, square bamboo for autumn, and speckled bamboo for winter.

Standing proudly in the north is the seven-bay-wide Mountain-Hugging Tower, the largest of all of the architectural structures in the garden. Low-rise rock gardens in front and on both sides of the tower serve to soften the visual impact of the massive building. The artificial hill right in front of the tower rises

6 meters (20 feet) tall, a typical rock garden for the summer, built entirely of lakebed stones. Below the hill, sparkling reflections in the pond create the illusion of larger space. A winding footbridge on the right side of the pond leads to a deep cave, where a skylight has been installed on the roof, which functions as a wind scoop to channel breezes from the pond into the cave, and keep the inside cool in hot summer. The grayish white of the southern facade contrasts nicely with the surrounding evergreens, offering a serene summer setting.

East of the tower rises a group of rock gardens built of yellow stones, and hence nicknamed Small Yellow Mountain. The stones have amazingly sharp edges, as cleanly made as though cut with an axe, which look

Fig. 225 *The rock garden in the Geyuan Garden at Yangzhou in autumn. The yellow rock provides a hard clear-cut outline, and adds to the autumnal atmosphere created by maple trees.*

Fig. 226 *The tall octagonal doorway in the Geyuan Garden, a Ming garden that fell into ruin and was then restored by a Qing official.*

226

Fig. 227 *The ground plan of the Geyuan Garden. Rockworks representing the four seasons surround the main scenic area, interspersed with buildings and plants.*

Fig. 228 *The deep cave is shady, a sharp contrast to the sunshine outside.*

Fig. 229 *The main scenic area to the west, with early spring foliage.*

Fig. 230 *The moon gate of the Geyuan Garden in spring. The standing stones and the bamboo provide an elegant visual context, built up of squares, circles and verticals.*

at their best in the autumn light. The artificial hill is divided into three peaks: western, southern, and central. Located on the summit of the central peak, the Cloud-Kissing Pavilion is the tallest and best-known landmark, overlooking the whole garden. The ancient landscapers were ingenious enough to have the hill face west, so that when the sun is going down, the leaves of the red maple trees planted below seem to set the hill aflame. It is an awe-inspiring sight.

When autumn has given way to winter, the rock garden at the southern wall is at its best. It is located in a semi-walled-in courtyard, in front of the Windy and Moonlit Hall in the southeast corner of the garden. Made from Xuan stones (full of quartz crystals) taken from the Anhui province, the stones have been carefully placed to create the impression of winter. These round, smooth, and whitish stones on the shady side

of the high wall help to create an illusion of blowing snow. In addition, twenty-four wind holes were carved into the southern wall. These holes function like a wind instrument, emitting rising and falling tones as the wind blows through, making the cold seem even colder. Several winter plum trees (*mei*) were planted close to the winter garden, and the scent of their flowers served to accentuate the winter view. Flanking the Windy and Moonlit Hall are two closed-in walls, complete with patterned window frames in the southern wall. This was where the owners of the garden used to drink wine and enjoy the view over the snow.

The ingenious use of uniquely shaped, colored, and textured stones, together with trees and plants, has culminated in what we see today—rock gardens focusing on different themes, and beautifully composed scenic vistas that change with each season.

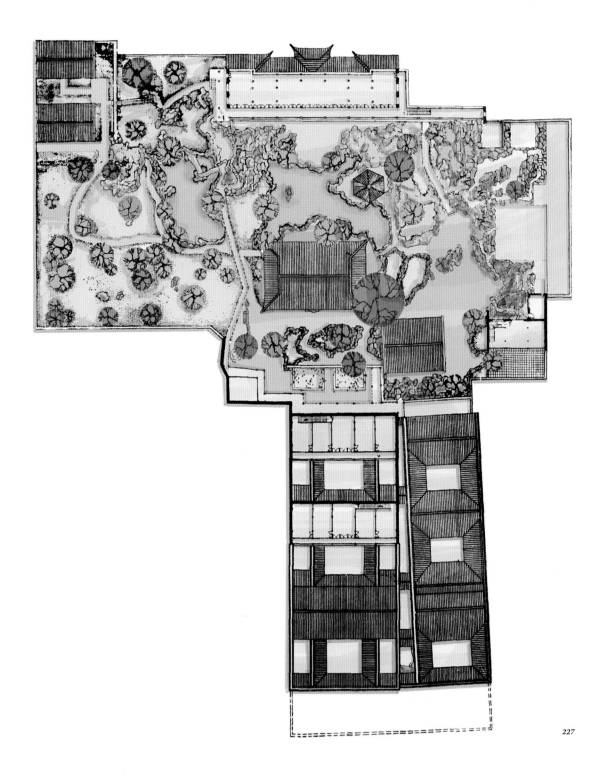

228

229

The Zhanyuan Garden

First built in the early Ming period, Zhanyuan Garden at Nanjing, in East China's Jiangsu province, has changed ownership several times over the past six hundred years. In 1958, it was rebuilt and enlarged, with the eastern and western sections combined into one, by using both traditional and modern landscaping methods typical of South and North China.

Zhanyuan Garden features a narrow, north-south strip of land, with the Jingmiao Hall, the main structure in the garden, as the dividing line between two enclosures: a small one in the south and a larger one to the north. This helps to compensate for any sense of narrowness. While both enclosures are filled with hills, waters, flowers, and trees, the south appears busy and a little noisy, while the north seems far away and quiet. The overall layout is centrally aligned, with all the buildings, cloisters, pavilions, and terraces placed along the perimeter of the site, so that more structures could fit in a small space, and yet would not look overcrowded.

The particular layout of the garden requires the scenic route to be closed and circular. Garden landscaping, especially in Chinese gardens, is, to some extent, the art of space. Not only should it focus on

Fig. 231 The Zhanyuan Garden is the only intact garden surviving from the Ming Dynasty in the City of Nanjing, Jiangsu province.

Fig. 232 The Jingmiao Hall, the main building of the Zhanyuan Garden, divides the garden into two parts, north and south.

fixed views and vistas, but equal attention needs to be paid to "linear" landscapes that visitors may admire while walking. That explains why the long corridor in the east winds its way past a series of small courtyards, from the small vestibule to the little veranda and flower hall, and finally to the wide open half-pavilion, thereby gradually evoking feelings of space.

Zhanyuan Garden is best known for its rock formations, particularly the three rock gardens in the north, south, and west of the garden. Built of more than 1,000 tons of selected Taihu rocks, the southern rocks are pieced together diagonally to emphasize their patterns and textures; to ensure maximum durability, rocks were laid overlapping each other vertically. The main body of the hill contains two layers, one with mud-coated stones, and the other with stone-coated mud, alternating to present a variety of contours. Cliffs, valleys, and footpaths all combine to create a feeling of nature. To avoid obstructing the view, shrubs and creepers are planted either in front of the rock garden, beside the lake, or in the valley. At the back of the rockwork, a forest of black pines, interspersed with

maples and gingkos, offers an air of mountain serenity, full of contrast and a dramatic change of seasonal colors. These ancient, towering trees also serve to screen off distracting elements outside the garden that do not match the beauty within. Architecturally, the south rock garden of Zhanyuan Garden is almost a perfect match for that of Huanxiu Mountain Villa in Suzhou.

Originally a rocky hill during the Ming Dynasty, the north rock garden is piled up with Taihu rocks. The footbridge over the deep valley, the level bridge close to water, and the massive, flat boulder projecting over water—all form a sharp contrast with the imposing stone wall standing at the back.

The water features of Zhanyuan Garden come in a variety of styles and sizes. While all the waterscapes are interlinked, they are visually divided into three sections, thereby forming three centers. The pool in the north is winding and labyrinthine, that in the south large and peaceful, and that in the east small but secluded—independent of each other, but connected together, to conjure a feeling of unfathomable mystery.

235

The Jichang Garden

In his *The Craft of Gardens*, Ji Cheng, a Ming Dynasty landscaper, argues that gardens are best located in woods or mountains; to create landscapes within the city proper is the last option. Although most private gardens are located within the city limits, Jichang Garden is an exception. Set between Mount Xi and Mount Hui west of the city of Wuxi, in east China's Jiangsu province, Jichang is in every way a woodland garden in the mountains, and a fine example of a unique rock garden as well.

Basically, the whole garden area can be divided into two sections: east and west. The eastern half consists mainly of pools and walkways by the water, where most architectural structures are clustered to take advantage of the mountain view. The western half comprises plants and rocks, seen as a continuation of those real mountains.

Jinhuiyi, a narrow pool running north to south in the eastern section, is an uninterrupted expanse of wide open space, and thereby provides visitors with enough distance to enjoy the finest view. Most scenic spots, not surprisingly, are scattered around the pool. The Happy Fish Pavilion, to the east of the pool, is a square-shaped pavilion with a roof of nine ridges and flying eaves,

Fig. 237 The Jichang Garden in Wuxi, Jiangsu province from the east, with Xishan Mountain and Xishan Temple, a "borrowed view," in the distance.

Fig. 238 Alternating shapes of aperture in the corridor in the south of the Jichang Garden allow a glimpse of the garden beyond.

239

240

where visitors can enjoy looking over the railings at the swimming fish below. A glance to the northwest from here will reveal a fine view of the pagoda atop Mount Xi in the far distance. Meanwhile, the pond, like a huge mirror, reflects wonderful images of the surrounding landscapes, including Mount Hui, thus creating an enhanced feeling of a larger space through the masterly use of a "borrowed view."

The fine rocks in the west section, the best part of the garden, are arranged as an artificial hill of less than 5 meters (16 feet), built of earth and interspersed with yellow stones. The head of the hill faces Mount Xi, and the tail points to Mount Hui—as if making a virtual connection between these two mountains. Walking on the three footpaths among the rocks, visitors are intended to marvel at the different illusions created by

the landscapers: steep cliffs and deep valleys, wooded trails, and waterside paths. Well proportioned to the pool, the rock garden forms a perfect contrast to the limpid reflections in the water.

A stream from a spring on Mount Hui flows through the rocks into the pool. As the water channel is exceptionally winding and curved, full of bends and falls, the stream gurgles and bubbles all the way down, hence the nickname, "Valley of Eight Notes."

In general, the success of Jichang Garden lies in its expert combination of natural landscapes and man-made wonders. Woods, mountains, spring water, and the "borrowed view" of Mount Hui and Xi—all of these endow the garden with a sublime charm, and help to make it a masterpiece of classical gardens in South China.

Fig. 239 The corridor in front of the Hanbi Pavilion in the east of the Jichang Garden.

Fig. 240 The Waterside Pavilion to the west bank of Jinhui Rivulet of the Jichang Garden. The axes of the garden converge and diverge here, a concise and effective design.

Fig. 241 When you enter the door facing the street, your eye is drawn to a small rockwork through the second round doorway. This design is used because the door is too near to the water and the space cannot accommodate a more usual design.

Fig. 242 The view of the garden from the west. The Zhiyu Kan, the main building on the bank, is spacious, offering an excellent view over the water.

The Yuyuan Garden

Located in the northeast of the Old City area of Shanghai, Yuyuan Garden was first built in the early 17th century, during the late Ming Dynasty. Famous for its numerous massive, historic buildings lavishly decorated in the traditional style, it is considered one of the finest examples of the Chinese merchants' gardens.

Covering a total area of 4.7 hectares, Yuyuan Garden consists of four major areas: west, east, middle, and the Inner Garden. Highlights of the west area include the Sansui Hall and the Grand Rockery. Splendid and spacious, the Sansui Hall, literally the Hall of Three Corn Ears, is the largest building in the garden, once a meeting place for wealthy merchants from Shanghai.

Created by Zhang Nanyang, a Ming Dynasty master rock garden builder from South China, the Grand Rockery rises 14 meters (45 feet), piled with as many as several thousand tons of yellow rocks from Wukang, home of the best-quality yellow rocks. The rockwork features rolling peaks, exotic flowers and trees, and a stunning pond, creating a spectacular landscape of woods and mountains. At its foot sits a pavilion, where visitors can get a bird's eye view of the whole garden. Another pavilion, standing high above the rocks, offers a clear view of the forests of sails and masts in the Pujiang River. Situated immediately next to Sansui Hall and facing the Grand Rockery from across the pond,

Fig. 243 The "wave-topped" dragon wall of the inner garden of the Yuyuan Garden in Shanghai.

Fig. 244 Outside to the north of the Yuhua Hall in the Yuyuan Garden. The hall was built as a viewing point for the Yulinglong Rock, with marvelous stones and rockwork.

244

245

Fig. 245 The Yulinglong is one of the three most famous rocks in South China, and the main focus of the Yuyuan Garden.

the Rolling Rain Tower looks best after the rain, when distant hills disappear behind shifting curtains of rain and mists tumble down from the roof of the terrace.

Heralding Spring Hall, the main building in the east area, is a spacious gathering place with painted beams and rafters. Opposite the hall stands a small, elegant theater stage, popularly known as "Fight and Sing Platform." Notably, half of the stage hangs over a small pond fed by a stream flowing from under a small pile of rocks southeast of the stage. The Hall of Harmony and Mildness, south of the theater stage, is a glass-enclosed, two-story building that houses a display of Ming-style furniture. With its front facing the mountains, and its back against the water, the hall is warm in winter and cool in summer.

Located south of the Entwined Dragon Bridge, the Inner Garden is fairly small, covering only 0.13 hectare. Elegant and compact, the architectural style is slightly different from the other areas in the garden. Rock

gardens, waterscapes, flowers, and trees are all carefully laid out to create beauty, peace, and greenery. Sunshine and Snow Hall, the principal hall of the Inner Garden, rises above a forest of grotesque peaks that face it. With careful observation, more than one hundred animal images can, it is said, be identified among the peaks.

Also noteworthy is the Nine Dragon Pool, installed southeast of the Peaceful Observation Hall of the Inner Garden. Hidden between the eastern and western walls of the pool are four dragon heads carved out of stone, clearly reflected in the water. In addition, the pool is fantastically shaped like the body of a dragon, hence the name. Built during the late Qing Dynasty, an ancient theater stage sits at the southern end of the Inner Garden. Lavishly embellished with lifelike wood carvings, the stage features a bell-shaped chamber that has been acoustically treated for perfect sound effects even without a microphone.

Figs. 246–247 Two doorways in the Yuyuan Garden.

Fig. 248 The waterscape in front of the Deyi Tower, the most spacious area in the garden. The zigzag bridge is close to the water; the rocks fixed to the piles supporting the bridge link visually to the stony landscape.

246

247

Fig. 249 *The buildings in the
Yuyuan Garden are magnificent,
with figures of the Eight
Immortals on the roof.*

Fig. 250 *Stone lions can be seen
at a number of entrances and in
front of main buildings.*

Fig. 251 *The pool between
the Cangbao Tower and the
Dianchun Hall, with the Shoin
Building on top of the rockwork
in the distance.*

The Keyuan Garden

Literally, Keyuan means "a garden not too bad for visiting," somewhat on the modest side. Covering an area of 0.22 hectare in the shape of a triangle, Keyuan Garden at Dongguan is, in fact, a splendid architectural work. Superbly landscaped and exquisitely designed, it epitomizes what historic gardens in South China's Guangdong province are all about.

The park contains numerous historic buildings, including traditional houses, villas, pavilions, courtyards, flower gardens, and studios, all skillfully joined together in a small area. All of the architectural structures feature smooth blue bricks with a simple yet classic design. Flowers and trees in the garden are carefully laid out with fine taste and discrimination, typical of the southern style.

Separated in the middle by a courtyard, the garden consists of two groups of buildings: southwest and northeast. Taken together, there are more than 130 doorways of various sizes and designs. Combined with the labyrinthine walkway and passages, they form an exciting maze of paths and trails.

A covered walkway winds around the whole garden, in the form of an eaves gallery in front of a building, or as a freestanding, circuitous corridor when away from buildings. Upon entering and walking through the hallway, visitors will marvel at the majestic mysterious landscape of a small pavilion called Bohong. Literally, Bohong means "peeling a lychee," suggesting that the pavilion was where scholars would gather to taste lychees.

Fig. 252 The buildings (often more than one story) in the Keyuan Garden in Guangdong province are linked to each other. Great attention has been paid to the detail of horizontal stone surfaces and to the careful use of plants.

Fig. 253 The Keting Pavilion on the Kehu Lake. The late Qing garden was made between 1850 and 1858, and later extended.

253

Ketang Hall, the main structure of the Keyuan Garden, has a ground floor lobby named Ke Studio paved with osmanthus-shaped slabs, hence the nickname the Sweet Osmanthus Hall. On top of the studio is mounted the Inviting Moon Tower, a four-story castlelike structure that rises 15.6 meters (51 feet), the highest point of the garden. On the top floor, visitors have a panoramic view of the city skyline and distant hills. Opposite the hall rises A Lion Jumping on a Terrace, a huge stone hill resembling a lion, with a terrace built in the middle.

West of the Ketang Hall is the Double Pure Chamber, another highlight of Keyuan Garden, where the garden owner used to recite poems. The name Double Pure, according to tradition, comes from the two landscapes in front of the chamber: the Delightful Green Bridge and the Curved Moonlit Pond. Architecturally, the chamber is H-shaped, with two spreading wings. The floor, ceiling, and windows all follow the same pattern and shape, an auspicious symbol and promise of good luck.

Behind the chamber is a small courtyard named Asking the Flowers, a place where the owner surrounded himself with flowers. The winding walkway leads visitors out of the courtyard and on toward the Sky in a Pot, a central open area with buildings on four sides, a great place to escape the summer heat, play chess or sip tea. And once outside, visitors will be rewarded with a relaxing view of Kehu Lake.

254

The Xiling Seal Engravers' Society

In addition to its spectacular world-class sites, the West Lake in Hangzhou has a number of beautiful private gardens around its shores, including the Xiling Seal Engravers' Society, although strictly speaking this small park is not a private garden, but a public place where artists can gather. Unlike other historic gardens, the Society was built by the premier landscapers of the early 20th century, whose unique style is both dynamic and inspiring. When the Society was first founded on Solitary Hill by a group of famous epigraphists in 1904, the 30th year of Qing Emperor Guangxu's reign (1875–1908), research on the art of bronze sculpture and stone inscription was at its peak. Covering a total area of over 7,000 square meters (75,300 square feet), with a floor space of nearly 2,000 square meters, (21,500 square feet), the Society is so named because it is located close to the Xiling Bridge. Fantastic cliffside inscriptions and exquisitely designed buildings dot this peaceful hillside, a rare example of the combination of the art of seal engraving and the art of the garden, which speaks volumes about the refined taste of both artists and landscapers.

At the entrance to the hill there is a marble gateway with a simple yet classic design. Beyond the gateway are a pavilion in honor of great sages and a library named Mountain and Rain. Further uphill, to the north, is the Fountain of Seals, so named because tradition has it that a fountain was unearthed by accident in 1911,

Fig. 256 The exquisite hillside park of the Xiling Seal Engravers' Society in Hangzhou, Zhejiang province. The pool dug into the rock below a stone tower at the top of the hill. The carving on the stone rockface reflects, as was planned, in the limpid water of the pool. This is one of the great 20th-century gardens of the world.

Fig. 257 The corridor to the east of the Baitang Hall, with inscriptions along the wall.

Highlights of Classical Chinese Gardens

257

*Figs. 258–259 Fine inscriptions
cut into the wall of the stone
cave.*

*Fig. 260 The stone room of classic
design, with the Jingtu Tower on
the top. Inside is an ancient and
precious stele.*

when the ancient walls were being repaired. Together
with Fountain of Leisure, Fountain of Meditation, and
Fountain of Scholars, they are collectively known as the
"Four Fountains of Xiling." Higher up stands the Four
Sunshines Tower, a courtyard that offers a fine view
of all four directions, including the West Lake in the
distance. The buildings are all carefully laid out around
an irregularly shaped pool within the courtyard. More
importantly, individual architectural structures are
neither connected by covered walkways, nor separated
by partition walls. Instead, buildings, caves, bamboo
groves, and trees interact with each other in such a way
as to create a natural landscape.

On a cliffside of the hill are inscribed four Chinese
characters: Xi Ling Yin She (literally, Xiling Seal
Engravers' Society). Flanking the inscribed tablet
on the east and west sides are multi-story buildings, including, most notably, the Stone Pagoda of
Avatamsaka Sutra that towers proudly above all the
rest. While it is true that pagodas are rarely found
in traditional Chinese gardens, the one erected here
successfully accentuates the vertical visual effect, pull-
ing all the architectural elements of the hill together.
Since the hill is only 30 meters (98 feet) high, the stone
pagoda, in fact, is less massive than it looks. Like the
stone inscriptions, the whole garden seems to have
been carved out of the hillside, highlighted with fine

details and brought to life with powerful images.

Equally noteworthy is the thoughtful arrangement
of plants: tall rhamnus trees and pines around the
stone pagoda, low-lying azaleas and box trees around
the pool, and bamboo groves on the hillsides. What
is more, the numerous seal cuttings, stone carvings,
inscribed couplets, and name plaques dramatically
enhance the visual landscape and sense of space.

On the whole, the buildings in the garden are
constructed in the traditional style, although in
places some structures do not conform to the Ming
and Qing Dynasty styles. Unlike many other historic
gardens, Xiling Society maintains the essence of
classical landscaping by working with the existing
topographical features, rather than remodeling what
is already there. Regrettably, although it has been
widely acclaimed as a masterpiece that should have
inspired a reformation of traditional garden making,
it failed to start a new trend.

Since the scenery of the West Lake is said to
resemble a long scroll of traditional Chinese water-ink
painting, the landscape of the Xiling Seal Engravers'
Society would appropriately be the elegant seal on
that painting. Yet with an area of no more than 0.33
hectare, remarkably, this small and unostentatious
park offers a breathtakingly panoramic view, and is
one of the very finest gardens.

Fig. 261 As you enter the gateway of the Xiling Seal Engravers' Society, the plan of the garden is carved in the style of a seal on the white wall to the right. In front, the garden rises through the trees, while a still pool almost fills the court to the left.

Fig. 262 The Xiaolonghong Opening cuts through the top of the hill to a silent and tranquil inner space detached from the chaotic world outside.

Fig. 263 To celebrate the 85th anniversary of the Seal Engravers' Society, a new generation of artists carved an elegant inscription on a stone cut into the shape of a large seal.

261

262

戊辰春
印人社
集同友
建社於
五周年

TIMELINE FOR DYNASTIC CHINA

Xia Dynasty	21st to 17th century B.C.
Shang Dynasty	1600–1046 B.C.
Zhou Dynasty	Western Zhou (1046–771 B.C.) Eastern Zhou 　　Spring and Autumn Period (770–476 B.C.) 　　Warring States Period (476–221 B.C.)
Qin Dynasty	221–206 B.C.
Han Dynasty	Western Han (206 B.C.–25 A.D.) Eastern Han (25–220)
Three Kingdoms Period	220–280
Jin Dynasty	Western Jin (265–317) Eastern Jin (317–420)
Northern and Southern Dynasties	Southern Dynasties (420–589) Northern Dynasties (386–581)
Sui Dynasty	581–618
Tang Dynasty	618–907
Five Dynasties and Ten States	Five Dynasties (907–960) Ten States (902–979)
Song Dynasty	Northern Song (960–1127) Southern Song (1127–1279)
Liao Dynasty	907–1125
Jin Dynasty	1115–1234
Yuan Dynasty	1206–1368
Ming Dynasty	1368–1644
Qing Dynasty	1616–1911

Photographers: Guo Guang, Ren Yuan, Mang Yu, Ma Wenxiao, Fang Xiaofeng, Li Shaobai, Li Jiang, Shao Zhong, Wu Dai, Zhou Suning, Zhou Meisheng, He Wei, Jiang Dafu, Jiang Chenming, Tan Ming, Sunfotos Photo Gallery, Phototime Photo Gallery, Panoramic Photo Gallary, Best View Stock Photo Gallary
English Translation: Ma Hongjun
Design: Zhang Yuhai

Fang, Xiaofeng.
[Great Chinese gardens]
The great gardens of China : history, concepts, techniques / Fang, Xiaofeng.—1st American ed.
p. cm.
"First published in 2010 in the United Kingdom as The great Chinese gardens by CYPI Press, Harrow Middlesex."
ISBN 978-1-58093-303-2 (hardcover)
1. Gardens, Chinese—Design. 2. Gardens—China—History. I. Title.
SB457.55.F36 2010
712.0951—dc22
2010011152

Printed in China

10 9 8 7 6 5 4 3 2 1
First American Edition

www.monacellipress.com